THE JEWISH FACT FINDER

YAFFA GANZ

THE JEWISH FACT FINDER

A Bookful of Important Torah Facts and Handy Jewish Information

Feldheim Publishers

Jerusalem □ New York

All transliteration in this book is according to the Ashkenazis pronunciation.
The Jewish Factfinder also appears in a separate edition using the Sefaradit pronunciation.

First Published 1988
Second, corrected edition 1995
Hardcover edition: ISBN 0-87306-447-x
Paperback edition: ISBN 0-87306-470-4

FELDHEIM PUBLISHERS
200 Airport Executive Park
Nanuet, NY 10954

POB 35002 / Jerusalem, Israel

Printed in Israel

Library of Congress Cataloging-in-Publication Data
Ganz, Yaffa,
The Jewish fact-finder: a bookful of important Torah facts and handy
Jewish information / by Yaffa Ganz.
p.   cm.
Bibliography: p.
Summary: Facts about Judaism are presented in over seventy lists
arranged into sections, such as "People in the Tanach," "The Holy
Books," "The Land of Israel," "The Holy Language," and "All Around the
Calendar."

1. Judaism — Outlines, syllabi, etc. — Juvenile literature.
[1. Judaism — Outlines, syllabi, etc.] I. Title.
BM573.G36 1988
296-dc 19
88-3969

10 9 8 7 6 5 4 3

In memory of my beloved teacher

הָרַב אֶלִיָהוּ ב״ר נַחוּם חַיִּים בְּלָאךְ

Rabbi Eliyahu ben HaRav Nachum Chayim Bloch

זכרונו לברכה

who taught at the

Hebrew Parochial School of Chicago.

He filled our hearts with love
for God, His Torah,
His people and His Land.
And he kindled in our minds the desire to learn.

Dear Reader,

If you sat your entire lifetime and did nothing but study Torah, although you might become very wise, you would still know only a fraction of what the Torah has to teach, and you would still have mastered but a tiny drop of Hashem's endless wisdom.

Nonetheless, each of us is commanded to learn as much as he or she possibly can, and each of us begins at the same beginning — with the letters of the Alef beis. We gather our information slowly, step by step; each new item is like another brick in a house we are trying to build. Bricks alone will not make a complete house, but without them, we have no house at all. So too, facts alone will not make us wise in the ways of Torah, but without them, there is no learning at all.

As we move on to more difficult and complicated subjects, there are often many important pieces of information we need to know, but which we don't have. And very often, they are hard to find.

Although no book can possibly include everything, this book is meant to give you, in a handy, easy form, the basic information which every Jew should know. It will not always explain things to you — you'll want your teacher for that — but it *will* help you find the facts you are looking for, quickly and simply. It will give you the "bricks" you can use to build your own House of Torah.

Sincerely,

Yaffa Ganz

Some important information about
THE JEWISH FACT FINDER

Differing opinions

In any book of Jewish information — be it facts, history, or halacha — the author must often choose between differing opinions and sources. Throughout this book, we have attempted to use the simplest and the most widely accepted information found in classical Jewish sources.

Calendars & dates

In THE JEWISH FACT FINDER, the years are numbered according to the Hebrew calendar. However, in all of Section H, *Time — All Around the Calendar*, both the Hebrew and the standard calendar dates are listed to help the reader coordinate both dating systems.

Counting years

There are different ways to "count years." In Biblical times, when one important event ended and a new one began and both took place in the same calendar year, that year was sometimes counted "twice" — once as part of the last event, and then again as part of the second event.

Hebrew pronunciation and transliteration

All transliteration in this book is according to the Sefaradit pronunciation. THE JEWISH FACT FINDER appears in a separate edition using the Ashkenazis pronunciation.

The Hebrew vowel *kamatz gadol* = the English letter *a* as in *paw*.
The Hebrew vowel *patach* = the English letter *a* as in the word *pa*.
The Hebrew vowel *kamatz katan* = the English letter *o* as in *corner*.
The Hebrew vowel *cholam* = the English letter *o* as in the word *row*.

Contents

A People in the Tanach, 13

B Mesora (Torah Sheb'al Peh) The Oral Law, 28

C Sifrey Kodesh — The Holy Books, 47

D The Mishkan and the Beis Hamikdash — The Tabernacle and the Holy Temple, 58

E Eretz Yisrael — The Land of Israel, 63

Miscellanea: Middos, Mitzvos, Melachos, Measurements and More..., *102*

Bibliography, *119*

People in the Tanach

A/1. Ten Generations from Adam to Noach

	YEAR BORN	YEAR DIED	YEARS LIVED
1. Adam אָדָם	1	930	930
2. Shes שֵׁת	130	1042	912
3. Enosh אֱנוֹשׁ	235	1140	905
4. Keynan קֵינָן	325	1235	910
5. Mahalalel מַהֲלַלְאֵל	395	1290	895
6. Yered יֶרֶד	460	1422	962
7. Chanoch חֲנוֹךְ	622	987	365
8. Mesushelach מְתוּשֶׁלַח	687	1656	969
9. Lemech לֶמֶךְ	874	1651	777
10. Noach נֹחַ	1056	2006	950

A/2. Ten Generations from Noach to Avraham

	YEAR BORN	YEAR DIED	YEARS LIVED
1. Shem שֵׁם	1558	2158	600
2. Arpachshad אַרְפַּכְשַׁד	1658	2096	438
3. Shelach שֶׁלַח	1693	2126	433
4. Ever עֵבֶר	1723	2187	464
5. Peleg פֶּלֶג	1757	1996	239
6. Re'u רְעוּ	1787	2026	239
7. Serug שְׂרוּג	1819	2049	230
8. Nachor נָחוֹר	1849	1997	148
9. Terach תֶּרַח	1878	2083	205
10. Avraham אַבְרָהָם	1948	2123	175

A/3. The Avos and the Imahos — the Patriarchs and the Matriarchs

Avraham — Sarah
אַבְרָהָם   שָׂרָה

Yitzchak — Rivkah
יִצְחָק   רִבְקָה

Yaakov — Rachel and Leah
יַעֲקֹב   רָחֵל וְלֵאָה

	YEAR BORN	YEAR DIED	YEARS LIVED
Avraham	1948	2123	175
Yitzchak	2048	2228	180
Yaakov	2108	2255	147
Sarah	1958	2085	127

Information concerning dates of birth and number of years lived for the other Matriarchs is not mentioned in the Torah, and there are many differing opinions in various midrashim.

A/4. The Shevatim — the Twelve Tribes
(The twelve sons of Yaakov Avinu and his wives)

Sons of Leah

Reuven	רְאוּבֵן
Shimon	שִׁמְעוֹן
Levi	לֵוִי
Yehuda	יְהוּדָה
Yissachar	יִשָּׂשכָר
Zevulun	זְבוּלוּן

Sons of Bilhah

Dan	דָּן
Naftali	נַפְתָּלִי

Sons of Zilpah

Gad	גָּד
Asher	אָשֵׁר

Sons of Rachel

Yosef*	יוֹסֵף
Efrayim	אֶפְרַיִם
Menashe	מְנַשֶּׁה
Binyamin	בִּנְיָמִין

---

* Because of Yaakov's blessing to Yosef, Yosef's tribe is counted as two, bearing the names of his sons Efrayim and Menashe (אֶפְרַיִם וּמְנַשֶּׁה).

A/5. Seven Generations from Avraham to Moshe

1. Avraham and Sarah
   אַבְרָהָם וְשָׂרָה

2. Yitzchak and Rivka
   יִצְחָק וְרִבְקָה

3. Yaakov and Leah
   יַעֲקֹב וְלֵאָה

4. Levi and Adina
   לֵוִי וַעֲדִינָה

5. Kehas (wife unknown)
   קְהָת

6. Amram and Yocheved
   עַמְרָם וְיוֹכֶבֶד

7. Moshe and Tzippora
   מֹשֶׁה וְצִפֹּרָה

Moshe was the twenty-sixth generation after Adam Harishon. He was born in the year 2368, and he died 120 years later in 2488.

A/6. From Avraham to King David

Avraham
אַבְרָהָם

Yitzchak
יִצְחָק

Yaakov
יַעֲקֹב

Yehuda
יְהוּדָה

Peretz
פֶּרֶץ

Chetzron
חֶצְרוֹן

Ram
רָם

Aminadav
עַמִּינָדָב

Nachshon
נַחְשׁוֹן

Salma
שַׂלְמָה

Boaz
בֹּעַז

Oved
עוֹבֵד

Yishai
יִשַׁי

David
דָּוִד

David Hamelech was the thirty-third generation after Adam Harishon. He was born in the year 2854, and died seventy years later in 2924.

A/7. Shoftim and Zekeynim — the Judges and the Elders

Before Moshe Rabbeinu died, God commanded him to appoint his student, Yehoshua bin Nun from the tribe of Efraim, as leader of the Jewish people. For 390 years, from the time the Jews entered Eretz Yisrael with Yehoshua until Shaul was appointed first King of Israel, the Jews were ruled by the Zekeynim (Elders) and the Shoftim (Judges). There were two Zekeynim and sixteen Shoftim.

	RULED	
Yehoshua יְהוֹשֻׁעַ בִּן נוּן	2488-2516	28 years

The two Zekeynim:

Kalev ben Yefuneh
כָּלֵב בֶּן יְפֻנֶּה

Pinchas ben Elazar Hakohen
פִּינְחָס בֶּן אֶלְעָזָר הַכֹּהֵן

The Shoftim

Osniel ben Kenaz עָתְנִיאֵל בֶּן קְנַז	2516-2556	40 years
Eyhud ben Gera אֵהוּד בֶּן גֵּרָא	2556-2636	80 years
Shamgar ben Anas שַׁמְגַּר בֶּן עֲנָת	2636	1 year
Devora Hanevia and Barak ben Avinoam דְּבוֹרָה הַנְּבִיאָה בָּרָק בֶּן אֲבִינֹעַם	2636-2676	40 years
Gidon ben Yoash גִּדְעוֹן בֶּן יוֹאָשׁ	2676-2716	40 years
Avimelech ben Gidon אֲבִימֶלֶךְ בֶּן גִּדְעוֹן	2716-2719	3 years
Tola ben Puah תּוֹלָע בֶּן פּוּאָה	2719-2742	23 years
Yair Hagiladi יָאִיר הַגִּלְעָדִי	2742-2764	22 years

The conquest of Israel by Amon took place in 2764. Amon oppressed them for eighteen years. There was no Shofet until the year 2781.

Yiftach Hagiladi יִפְתָּח הַגִּלְעָדִי	2781-2787	6 years
Ivtzan (Boaz) אִבְצָן (בֹּעַז)	2787-2793	7 years
Eylon Hazevuloni אֵילוֹן הַזְּבוּלֹנִי	2793-2803	10 years
Avdon ben Hillel עַבְדּוֹן בֶּן הִלֵּל	2803-2811	8 years
Shimshon שִׁמְשׁוֹן	2811-2831	20 years
Eli Hakohen עֵלִי הַכֹּהֵן	2831-2870	40 years
Shemuel Hanavi שְׁמוּאֵל הַנָּבִיא	2871-2882	11 years

A/8. Melachim — the Kings

	RULED	
1. Shaul Hamelech שָׁאוּל הַמֶּלֶךְ	2882-2884	2 years (Other opinions believe he ruled either 17 or 20 years.)

For five years after Shaul's reign, there was no king. There are differing opinions as to the exact chronology of this period.

2. Ish Boshes ben Shaul אִישׁ בּשֶׁת בֶּן שָׁאוּל	2889-2891	2 years
3. David Hamelech דָּוִד הַמֶּלֶךְ	For 7 ½ years he ruled in Chevron over his tribe — Yehudah. 2884-2892 For 33 years he ruled as king of all Israel in Jerusalem. 2892-2924	
4. Shlomo Hamelech שְׁלֹמֹה הַמֶּלֶךְ	2924-2964	40 years

Yehuda V'Yisrael — The Kingdoms of Judah and Israel

After the death of Shlomo Hamelech, the kingdom was divided into two — the southern Kingdom of Judah, which included the two tribes Yehuda and Binyamin; and the northern Kingdom of Israel, which included the other ten tribes.

Malchey Yehuda – the Kings of Judah

		RULED
Rechav'am ben Shlomo	רְחַבְעָם	17 years
Aviya ben Rechav'am	אֲבִיָּה	3 years
Asa ben Aviya	אָסָא	41 years
Yehoshafat ben Assa	יְהוֹשָׁפָט	25 years
Yehoram ben Yehoshafat	יְהוֹרָם	8 years
Achazyahu ben Yehoram	אֲחַזְיָהוּ	1 year
Asalya bas Omri	עֲתַלְיָה	6 years
Yehoash ben Achazyahu	יְהוֹאָשׁ	40 years
Amatzya ben Yehoash	אֲמַצְיָה	29 years
Uziyahu ben Amatzya	עֻזִיָּהוּ	52 years
Yosam ben Uziyahu	יוֹתָם	16 years
Achaz ben Yosam	אָחָז	16 years
Chizkiyahu ben Achaz	חִזְקִיָּהוּ	29 years
Menashe ben Chizkiyahu	מְנַשֶּׁה	55 years
Amon ben Menashe	אָמוֹן	2 years
Yoshiyahu ben Amon	יֹאשִׁיָּהוּ	31 years
Yehoachaz ben Yoshiyahu	יְהוֹאָחָז	3 months
Yehoyakim ben Yoshiyahu	יְהוֹיָקִים	11 years
Yehoyachin ben Yoshiyahu	יְהוֹיָכִין	3 months
Tzidkiyahu ben Yoshiyahu	צִדְקִיָּהוּ	11 years

On the Ninth of Av in the year 3338, during the reign of Tzidkiyahu, the First Beis Hamikdash was destroyed by the Babylonians and Galus Bavel — the Babylonian Exile — began.

Malchey Yisrael – the Kings of Israel

		RULED
Yarov'am ben Nevat	יָרׇבְעָם	22 years
Nadav ben Yarov'am	נָדָב	2 years
Ba'sha ben Achiya	בַּעְשָׁה	24 years
Eyla ben Ba'sha	אֵלָה	2 years
Zimri	זִמְרִי	7 days
Omri	עׇמְרִי	12 years
Achav ben Omri	אַחְאָב	22 years
Achazyahu ben Achav	אֲחַזְיָהוּ	2 years
Yehoram ben Achav	יְהוֹרָם	12 years
Yehu ben Nimshi	יֵהוּא	28 years
Yehoachaz ben Yehu	יְהוֹאָחׇז	17 years
Yehoash ben Yehoachaz	יְהוֹאָשׁ	16 years
Yarov'am ben Yehoash	יָרׇבְעָם	41 years
Zecharyahu ben Yarov'am	זְכַרְיָהוּ	6 months
Shallum ben Yavesh	שַׁלּוּם	1 month
Menachem ben Gadi	מְנַחֵם	10 years
Pekachya ben Menachem	פְּקַחְיָה	2 years
Pekach ben Remalyahu	פֶּקַח	20 years
Hosheya ben Eyla	הוֹשֵׁעַ	18 years

In the year 3187, the tribes of Reuven, Gad, and half the tribe of Menashe were exiled.
In 3205, the remaining tribes from the Kingdom of Israel were exiled. Together, these are known as the Ten Lost Tribes.

A/9. Neviim —
The Forty-Eight Prophets

The Jews received the Torah in the year 2448. From the time of Avraham Avinu, until 1000 years after the Giving of the Torah, there were prophets in Israel. During this time, hundreds of thousands of Jews reached the level of prophecy, but the names of only forty-eight prophets have been passed down to us through the Tanach. Only their teachings were necessary for the Jewish people to know and learn from for all time.

1. Avraham
   אַבְרָהָם

2. Yitzchak
   יִצְחָק

3. Yaakov
   יַעֲקֹב

4. Moshe Rabbeinu
   משֶׁה רַבֵּנוּ

5. Aharon Hakohen
   אַהֲרֹן הַכֹּהֵן

6. Yehoshua
   יְהוֹשֻׁעַ

7. Pinchas
   פִּינְחָס

8. Elkana
   אֶלְקָנָה

9. Eli Hakohen
   עֵלִי הַכֹּהֵן

10. Shemuel Haramasi
    שְׁמוּאֵל הָרָמָתִי

11. Gad Hachozeh
    גָּד הַחוֹזֶה

12. Nassan Hanavi
    נָתָן הַנָּבִיא

13. David Hamelech
    דָּוִד הַמֶּלֶךְ

14. Achiya Hashiloni
    אֲחִיָּה הַשִּׁילוֹנִי

15. Shlomo Hamelech
    שְׁלֹמֹה הַמֶּלֶךְ

16. Iddo Hachozeh
    עִדּוֹ הַחוֹזֶה

17. Eliyahu Hanavi
    אֵלִיָּהוּ הַנָּבִיא

18. Michayhu ben Yimla
    מִיכָיְהוּ בֶּן יִמְלָא

19. Ovadya
    עוֹבַדְיָה

20. Chanani Haroeh
    חֲנָנִי הָרוֹאֶה

21. Yehu ben Chanani
    יֵהוּא בֶּן חֲנָנִי

22. Azaryahu ben Oded
    עֲזַרְיָהוּ בֶּן עוֹדֵד

23. Yachaziel Halevi
    יַחֲזִיאֵל הַלֵּוִי

24. Eliezer ben Dodavahu
    אֱלִיעֶזֶר בֶּן דּוֹדָוָהוּ

25. Elisha ben Shafat
    אֱלִישָׁע בֶּן שָׁפָט

26. Yona ben Amittai
    יוֹנָה בֶּן אֲמִתַּי

continued on next page

27. Hoshea ben B'eri
הוֹשֵׁעַ בֶּן בְּאֵרִי

28. Zecharya ben Yehoyada Hakohen
זְכַרְיָה בֶּן יְהוֹיָדָע הַכֹּהֵן

29. Amos
עָמוֹס

30. Amotz
אָמוֹץ

31. Yishayahu ben Amotz
יְשַׁעְיָהוּ בֶּן אָמוֹץ

32. Micha
מִיכָה

33. Yoel ben Pesuel
יוֹאֵל בֶּן פְּתוּאֵל

34. Nachum Haelkoshi
נַחוּם הָאֶלְקוֹשִׁי

35. Uriyahu ben Shemayahu
אוּרִיָּהוּ בֶּן שְׁמַעְיָהוּ

36. Chavakuk
חֲבַקּוּק

37. Tzefanya ben Kushi
צְפַנְיָה בֶּן כּוּשִׁי

38. Yirmeyahu ben Chilkiyahu
יִרְמְיָהוּ בֶּן חִלְקִיָּהוּ

39. Yechezkel ben Buzi Hakohen
יְחֶזְקֵאל בֶּן בּוּזִי הַכֹּהֵן

40. Neria
נֵרִיָּה

41. Baruch ben Neria
בָּרוּךְ בֶּן נֵרִיָּה

42. Daniel Ish Chamudos
דָּנִיֵּאל אִישׁ חֲמוּדוֹת

43. Seraya
שְׂרָיָה

44. Machseya
מַחְסֵיָה

45. Mordechai
מָרְדְּכַי

46. Chaggai
חַגַּי

47. Zecharya
זְכַרְיָה

48. Malachi
מַלְאָכִי

A/10. Nevios —
The Seven Prophetesses

Sarah
שָׂרָה

Miriam
מִרְיָם

Devora
דְּבוֹרָה

Channa
חַנָּה

Avigayil
אֲבִיגַיִל

Chulda
חֻלְדָּה

Esther
אֶסְתֵּר

B Mesora (Torah Sheb'al Peh) The Oral Law

B/1. Mesora —
the Chain of Tradition

The Torah was passed down from

Sinai

to

Moshe

to

Yehoshua

to

the Zekeynim — the Elders

to

the Neviim — the Prophets

to

Anshey Knesses Hagedola — Men of the Great

Assembly

B/2. Anshey Knesses Hagedola — the Men of the Great Assembly
(c. 3350-3450)

The Anshey Knesses Hagedola consisted of 120 prophets, elders, scholars and great rabbis who served as the leaders of the Jewish people during the period between the destruction of the First Beis Hamikdash and the beginning of the Second Beis Hamikdash. According to some opinions, they continued to meet for eight generations. The following were among the 120 members of the Anshey Knesses Hagedola.

Ezra Hasofer

Chagai the Prophet

Zecharya the Prophet

Malachi the Prophet

Mordechai Hayehudi

Nechemya

Yehoshua ben Yehotzadak

Zerubavel ben Shaltiel

Daniel

Chananya

Mishael

Azarya

Shimon Hatzadik was among the last of the Anshey Knesses Hagedola and Antigonus Ish Socho was his student.

B/3. Zugos — the "Pairs" of Sages
(c. 3500-3750)

The Zugos are the pairs of sages who headed
the Sanhedrin — the Supreme Court — for
approximately 300 years after the Anshey
Knesses Hagedola. The first sage was the Nasi —
the president or head of the Sanhedrin. The
second was the Av Beis Din — the vice-
president.

Yosi ben Yoezer and Yosi ben Yochanan	c. 3500
Yehoshua ben Perachya and Nitai Ha'arbeyli	c. 3560
Yehuda ben Tabai and Shimon ben Shatach	c. 3621
Shemaya and Avatalyon	c. 3722
Hillel and Shammai	c. 3728

B/4. Tannaim (c. 3450-4000)

Tannaim is the name given to all the sages during the period of the Second Beis Hamikdash until the time of Rabi Yehuda Hanasi and the completion of the Mishna. "Tanna" is from the Aramaic word "to teach," for they taught the Oral Law.

The following is only a partial listing of the more than one hundred Tannaim who are mentioned in the Mishna and the Talmud. Nor are they all in exact chronological order. Many Tannaim spanned more than one generation.

a. Tannaim during Bayis Sheyni (c. 3450-3830)

Rabban Shimon ben Hillel Hazakeyn

Rabi Nechunya ben Hakanah

Rabi Pinchas

Rabi Yochanan ben Bag Bag

Nachum Halavlar

Rabi Yehoshua ben Gamla, Kohen Gadol

Rabban Gamliel Hazakeyn

Shemuel Hakatan

Rabban Shimon ben Gamliel Hazakeyn

Rabi Tzadok

Rabban Yochanan ben Zakkai —
N'si HaSanhedrin (Head of the Sanhedrin)

Churban Bayis Sheyni — the destruction of the Second Temple — occurred on Tisha B'Av in the year 3828 during the time of Rabban Yochanan ben Zakkai.

Rabi Eliezer Hamodai

Rabi Chanina ben Dosa

b. First generation of Tannaim after the Churban (c. 3830-3860)

Rabban Gamliel Hasheyni of Yavneh — N'si HaSanhedrin

Rabi Eliezer ben Hurkonus

Rabi Yehoshua ben Chananya

Rabi Yossi Hagalili Hakohen

Rabi Shimon ben Nesanel

Rabi Elazar ben Arach

Abba Shaul

Rabi Elazar ben Azarya Hakohen

Rabi Chalafta

Nachum Ish Gam Zu

c. Second generation of Tannaim after the Churban (c. 3860-3900)

Rabi Tarfon Hakohen

Rabi Akiva ben Yosef

Rabi Yishmael

Rabi Yehoshua ben Karcha

Unkelos Hager

Shimon ben Azai

Shimon ben Zoma

continued on next page

d. Third generation of Tannaim after the Churban (c. 3900-4000)

Rabban Shimon ben Gamliel — N'si HaSanhedrin

Rabi Meir

Rabi Yosi ben Chalafta

Rabi Yehuda bar Ilai

Rabi Shimon bar Yochai

Rabi Elazar ben Rabi Shimon

Rabi Pinchas ben Yair

Rabi Nassan HaBavli

Rabi Yochanan Hasandlar

e. Fourth and fifth generations of Tannaim after the Churban (c. 4000)

Rabi Yehuda Hanasi (Rabbeinu Hakadosh) He codified the Mishna.

Rabi Chanina bar Chama

Rabban Gamliel Hashlishi

Rabi Yehuda ben Teyma

Avuha D'Shemuel

Rabi Chiya

Rabi Oshiya

Rabi Yehoshua ben Levi

B/5. Amoraim

After the period of the Tannaim, the next group of teachers, rabbis and sages were called Amoraim. The "Amora" was the sage who "spoke" about and explained the teachings of the Tannaim.

There were more than eighteen hundred Amoraim. They lived in both Eretz Yisrael and in Babylonia, which had become a center of Jewish life and learning. The following is a partial listing of some of the better known Amoraim.

In Eretz Yisrael: the period of the Amoraim was from c. 4000-4150.

In Babylonia: the period of the Amoraim was from c. 4000-4260.

ERETZ YISRAEL	BAVEL (BABYLONIA)
First Generation **c. 4000**	
Rabi Yochanan	Rav
Rabi Shimon ben Lakish (Reysh Lakish)	Shemuel
Rabi Yanai	Rav Ada bar Ahava

continued on next page

ERETZ YISRAEL	BAVEL (BABYLONIA)
Second Generation **c. 4039**	
Rabi Ami and Rabi Asi	Rav Huna
Rabi Yosi bar Chanina	Rav Yehuda bar Yechezkel
Rabi Chiya bar Abba	Rav Nachman bar Yaakov
Rabi Shemuel bar Nachmeyni	Rav Sheshes
Rabi Yehuda N'siah	Rav Shimi
	Rav Kahana the First
	Rav Yirmiya bar Abba
	Rav Hammuna
	Rav Ami and Rav Asi
	Raba bar Avuhu
Third Generation **c. 4060**	
Rabi Avuhu	Rav Chisda
Rabi Zeyra	Raba bar Nachmeyni (known as Raba)
Rabi Dimi	Rav Yosef
Ravin	Ulah
Rabi Yirmiya	Rav Yitzchak b'rey d'Rav Yehuda
	Rav Kahana the Second
Fourth Generation **c. 4085**	
Rabi Yosi bar Zavda	Abayey
Rabi Chaggai	Rava
Rabi Yosi bar Avin	Rav Sechora
	Rav Safra

ERETZ YISRAEL	BAVEL (BABYLONIA)
Fifth Generation **c. 4118**	
Hillel Hanasi	Rav Nachman bar Yitzchak
	Rav Papa
	Rav Zvid
	Rav Huna b'rey D'Rabi Yehoshua
	Rav Ika
	Rav Acha
	Ameymar

The Talmud Yerushalmi was completed in the year 4128 by Rabi Yochanan.

Sixth Generation **c. 4150**	
	Rav Ashi
	Mar Zutra
	Ravina the First
	Rav Kahana the Third
Seventh Generation **c. 4187**	
	M'reymar
	Ravina the Second
	Mar bar Rav Ashi

The Babylonian Talmud was completed in the year 4260 by Ravina and Rav Ashi.
There were forty generations from Moshe Rabbeinu until Rav Ashi.

B/6. Savoraim in Babylonia
(c. 4260-4450)

The next group of sages were called Savoraim because they neither added to nor subtracted from the words of the Talmud. They only further explained ("savra") the teachings of the sages who lived before them. The following is a partial listing of the best known Savoraim.

First Generation

Raba bar Yosef

Rav Yosi

Second Generation

Rav Tachlifa

Rav Simona

Rav Eyna

Third Generation

Rav Ravai Meyrov

Rav Mari

Rav Chanina

Fourth Generation

Rav Yitzchak

Fifth Generation

Mar Huna

Mar Rava

Rav Shishna

Rav Busai

B/7. Geonim in Babylonia
(c. 4450-4800)

The heads of the famous yeshivos were called Geonim — great scholars.

Rav Chanina Gaon

Rav Neturai Gaon

Rav Yaakov Gaon

Rav Achai Gaon

Mar Yehudai Gaon

Rav Natronai Gaon

Rav Amram Gaon

Rav Saadya Gaon

Rav Shrira Gaon

Rav Hai Gaon

B/8. Rishonim (c. 4800-5200)

The following is a partial listing of the most famous rabbis and teachers of the period of the Rishonim. Many of them became known by either the acronym of their name or the title of their most famous work (in parentheses). The main centers of Jewish life and learning were in Spain, Provence, France, Germany and Italy.

In Spain

Rabi Yitzchak Alfasi (Rif)

Rabi Yehuda Halevi

Rabi Avraham Ibn Ezra

Rabi Moshe ben Maimon (Rambam)

Rabi Moshe ben Nachman (Ramban)

Rabi Meir Halevi Abulafiya (HaRama)

Rabbeinu Yona Hechassid of Gerona

Rabbeinu Bechayeh ben Asher

Ish Halevi (Hachinuch)

Rabbeinu Shlomo ben Aderes (HaRashba)

Rabbeinu Asher bar Yechiel (HaRosh)

Rabbeinu Yaakov ben Asher (Baal Haturim)

Rabbeinu Nissim bar Reuven (HaRan)

Rabi David ben Yosef (Avudraham)

Rabi Yom Tov ben Avraham (HaRitva)

Rabi Yitzchak Avuhav

In France

Rabi Shlomo Yitzchaki (Rashi)

Rabi Shemuel bar Meir (Rashbam)

Rabi Yaakov bar Meir (Rabbeinu Tam)

Rabi Yitzchak bar Shmuel (Ri Hazakeyn)

Rabi Yechiel mi'Paris

Rabi Eliezar of Touche

In Provence (an independent domain)

Rabi Zerachya Halevi (Ba'al Hamaor)

Rabi Avraham bar David (Ra'avad)

Rabi Menachem bar Shlomo (Hameiri)

Rabi David Kimchi (Radak)

Rabi Levi bar Gershon (Ralbag)

In Germany

Rabbeinu Gershom Maor Hagola

Rabi Yehuda Hechassid

Rabbeinu Meir ben Baruch (Maharam mi'Rottenburg)

In Italy

Rabi Nassan ben Yechiel of Rome (He'aruch)

Rabi Menachem ben Binyamin of Rikanti (HaRikanti)

B/9. Acharonim (c. 5200-5600)

This is a partial chronological listing of some of the most famous rabbis from the year 5200 until the year 5600 — approximately one hundred and fifty years ago.

Rabi Yisrael bar Pesachya Iserlin

Rabi Eliyahu Mizrachi (commentary on Torah)

Don Yitzchak Abarbanel (commentary on Torah)

Rabi Yitzchak Arama (Akeydas Yitzchak)

Rabi Ovadya mi'Bertinoro (commentary on Mishna)

Rabi Yaakov bar Shlomo Chaviv (Ein Yaakov)

Rabi Ovadya Zafroni (Seforno)

Rabi Yosef Karo (Shulchan Aruch)

Rabi Moshe Alsheych (commentary on Torah)

Rabi Moshe Cordova (Tomer Devora)

Rabi Shlomo Alkavetz Halevi (Lecha Dodi)

Rabi David ben Zimra (HaRadvaz)

Rabi Bezalel Ashkenazi (Shita Mekubetzes)

Rabbeinu Harav Yitzchak Luria (HaAri)

Rabi Chaim Vital

Rabbeinu Moshe Isserles (HaRama)

Rabi Shlomo Luria Ashkenazi (Hamaharshal)

Rabi Yehuda Loewe of Prague (Maharal)

Rabi Yishayahu Halevi Horovitz (HaShela)

Rabi Meir (Maharam mi'Lublin)

Rabi Shemuel Eliezer Halevi Eideliss (Maharsha)

Rabi Yoel Sirkiss (Bach)

Rabi Yom Tov Lipman (Tosfos Yom Tov)

Rabi David Av Beis Din of Levov (HaTaz)

Rabi Shabsai ben Rav Meir Hakohen (Shach)

Rabi Avraham Evli Halevi (Magen Avraham)

Rabi Shabsai Shtrum (Sifsei Chachamim)

Rabi Yehuda Hechassid

Rabi Chaim ben Atar (Or Hachaim)

Rabi Moshe Chaim Luzzatto (Mesillas Yesharim)

Rabi Yaakov Yehoshua mi'Krakow
(Pnei Yehoshua)

Rabi Yisrael ben Eliezer (Ba'al Shem Tov)

Rabi Aryeh Leib ben Reb Asher (Sha'agas Aryeh)

Rabi Yonasan Eibishitz (Tumim)

Rabi Yaakov Emden (HaYavetz)

Rabi Yosef Te'umim (Pri Megadim)

Rabi Yechezkel Halevi Landau (Noda
Beyehuda)

Rabi Shalom Sharaabi from Yemen

Rabi Eliahu bar Shlomo Zalman (Vilna Gaon)

Rabi Chaim Yosef David Azulai (Chidda)

Rabi Aryeh Leib Hakohen Heller (Ketzos
Hachoshen)

Rabi Avraham Danzig (Chayey Adam)

Rabi Chaim of Volozhin

Rabi Akiva Eiger

Rabi Moshe Sofer (Chassam Sofer)

B/10. The Chassidic Movement — the Ba'al Shem Tov and his Disciples

Rabi Yisrael ben Eliezer (the Ba'al Shem Tov or BESHT) was the founder of the Chassidic movement in Europe in the 1700s.
The following are some of the more famous Chassidic dynasties which still exist today.

Rabi Dov Ber, Maggid of Mezritch, was the Ba'al Shem Tov's successor.

Dynasty	Founder
Skver	Rabi Nachum of Chernobel
Stolin	Rabi Aharon Hagadol of Karlin
Chabad (Lubavitch)	Rabi Shneur Zalman of Liadi
Breslov	Rabi Nachman of Breslov
Sadiger, Boyan	Rabi Yisrael of Rizin
Satmar	Rabi Moshe Teitelbaum of Uhel
Vishnitz	Rabi Menachem Mendel of Kosov
Belze	Rabi Sar Shalom Rokeach
Gur	Rabi Yitzchak Meir Alter
Bobov, Kloizenberg	Rabi Chaim Halbershtam of Tzanz
Slonim	Rabi Avraham of Slonim
Modzitz	Rabi Yisrael of Modzitz
Zlotchov, Zvil	Rabi Yechiel Michel of Zlotchov

Other famous Chassidic Rebbes

Rabi Elimelech of Lizensk
Rabi Levi Yitzchak of Berditchev
Rabi Baruch of Mezibuz
Rabi Yaakov Yitzchak, the Seer of Lublin
Rabi Menachem Mendel of Kotzk
Rabi Tzadok Hakohen of Lublin

B/11. The Yeshiva Movement

The Yeshiva movement is a direct continuation of the great Torah academies of learning which flourished in Eretz Yisrael and Babylonia in the Talmudic and Geonic periods. Particularly in Lithuania, but also throughout Europe, these Torah institutions became very popular. The following is a list of towns which hosted some of the major yeshivos before World War II. After the Holocaust, many were reestablished in Israel and America by surviving rabbis and students.

Baranovitch

Bialostok

Brisk

Grodno

Kamenitz

Kletsk

Lubavitch

Lublin

Mir

Navahrdok

Pressburg

Radin

Slobodka

Telshe

Vilna

Volozhin

B/12. The Mussar Movement

The Mussar movement began in Lithuania in the nineteenth century. It is a system of teaching which stresses ethical and moral self-improvement to its students. The following is a list of founders of the movement.

Rabi Yisrael Salanter — founder of the Mussar movement

Rabi Itzel Blazer — successor to Rabi Salanter

Rabi Naftali of Amsterdam — a prime student of Rabi Salanter and perpetuator of his teachings

Rabi Simcha Zissel Ziv — founder of the Kelm mussar system

Rabi Nassan Tzvi Finkel — founder of the Slabodker mussar system

Rabi Yosef Horowitz — founder of the Navahrdoker mussar system

C Sifrey Kodesh — The Holy Books

1. TANACH — THE TWENTY-FOUR BOOKS OF THE BIBLE

2. CHUMASH AND PARSHIYOS — THE FIVE BOOKS
   OF MOSES AND THEIR SECTIONS

3. SHISHA SIDRAY MISHNA — THE SIX SECTIONS
   OF THE MISHNA

4. THE TALMUD (GEMARRA)

5. RAMBAM — MISHNEH TORAH (HAYAD HACHAZAKA)

6. SHULCHAN ARUCH — THE CODE OF JEWISH LAW

C/1. Tanach / סִפְרֵי הַתַּנַ"ךְ / the Twenty-Four Books of the Bible

The twenty-four books of the Bible are referred to as the Torah Shebichsav — the Written Law. The order presented here is the order listed in the Talmud (Bava Basra 14b).

The Torah / חֲמִשָּׁה חֻמְשֵׁי תּוֹרָה
The Five Books of Moses

1. Bereishis
   בְּרֵאשִׁית

2. Shemos
   שְׁמוֹת

3. Vayikra
   וַיִּקְרָא

4. Bemidbar
   בְּמִדְבַּר

5. Devarim
   דְּבָרִים

Neviim / נְבִיאִים
The Prophets

6. Yehoshua
   יְהוֹשֻׁעַ

7. Shoftim
   שׁוֹפְטִים

8. Shemuel (Alef and Beis)
   שְׁמוּאֵל

9. Melachim (Alef and Beis)
   מְלָכִים

10. Yirmeyahu
    יִרְמְיָהוּ

11. Yechezkel
    יְחֶזְקֵאל

12. Yishayahu
    יְשַׁעְיָהוּ

13. Trey Assar (The Twelve Prophets)
תְּרֵי עָשָׂר

Hoshea	Yona	Tzefanya
הוֹשֵׁעַ	יוֹנָה	צְפַנְיָה
Yoel	Micha	Chaggai
יוֹאֵל	מִיכָה	חַגַּי
Amos	Nachum	Zecharya
עָמוֹס	נַחוּם	זְכַרְיָה
Ovadya	Chavakuk	Malachi
עוֹבַדְיָה	חֲבַקּוּק	מַלְאָכִי

Kesuvim / כְּתוּבִים
The Writings

14. Ruth
רוּת

15. Tehillim (Psalms)
תְּהִלִּים

16. Iyov (Job)
אִיּוֹב

17. Mishley (Proverbs)
מִשְׁלֵי

18. Koheles
קֹהֶלֶת

19. Shir Hashirim (Song of Songs)
שִׁיר הַשִּׁירִים

20. Eicha
אֵיכָה

21. Daniel
דָּנִיֵּאל

22. Esther
אֶסְתֵּר

23. Ezra/Nechemya
עֶזְרָא/נְחֶמְיָה

24. Divrey Hayamim (Chronicles)
דִּבְרֵי הַיָּמִים

C/2. Chumash and Parshiyos — the Five Books of Moses and their Sections

BEREISHIS / בְּרֵאשִׁית

Bereishis בְּרֵאשִׁית	Chayey Sarah חַיֵּי שָׂרָה	Vayeyshev וַיֵּשֶׁב
Noach נֹחַ	Toldos תּוֹלְדֹת	Mikeytz מִקֵּץ
Lech Lecha לֶךְ לְךָ	Vayeytzey וַיֵּצֵא	Vayigash וַיִּגַּשׁ
Vayera וַיֵּרָא	Vayishlach וַיִּשְׁלַח	Vayechi וַיְחִי

SHEMOS / שְׁמוֹת

Shemos שְׁמוֹת	Yisro יִתְרוֹ	Ki Sisaw כִּי תִשָּׂא
Va'eyra וָאֵרָא	Mishpatim מִשְׁפָּטִים	Vayakhel וַיַּקְהֵל
Bo בֹּא	Teruma תְּרוּמָה	Pekudey פְקוּדֵי
Beshalach בְּשַׁלַּח	Tetzaveh תְּצַוֶּה	

VAYIKRA / וַיִּקְרָא

Vayikra וַיִּקְרָא	Metzora מְצֹרָע	Behar בְּהַר
Tzav צַו	Acharey Mos אַחֲרֵי מוֹת	Bechukosai בְּחֻקֹּתַי
Shemini שְׁמִינִי	Kedoshim קְדֹשִׁים	
Sazriya תַזְרִיעַ	Emor אֱמֹר	

BEMIDBAR / בְּמִדְבַּר

Bemidbar	Korach	Mattos
בְּמִדְבַּר	קֹרַח	מַטּוֹת
Naso	Chukas	Mas'ai
נָשֹׁא	חֻקַּת	מַסְעֵי
Beha'aloscha	Balak	
בְּהַעֲלֹתְךָ	בָּלָק	
Shelach	Pinchas	
שְׁלַח	פִּינְחָס	

DEVARIM / דְּבָרִים

Devarim	Shoftim	Vayelech
דְּבָרִים	שֹׁפְטִים	וַיֵּלֶךְ
Ve'eschanan	Ki Seytzey	Ha'azinu
וָאֶתְחַנַּן	כִּי תֵצֵא	הַאֲזִינוּ
Eykev	Ki Savoh	Vezos Haberachah
עֵקֶב	כִּי תָבוֹא	וְזֹאת הַבְּרָכָה
R'ay	Nitzavim	
רְאֵה	נִצָּבִים	

C/3. Shisha Sidray Mishna — the Six Sections of the Mishna

The Mishna is the summary of the Torah Sheb'al Peh — the Oral Law as set down by the Tannaim and summarized by Rabi Yehuda Hanasi. There are six sections in the Mishna. Each is divided into tractates called masechtos and each masechta is further divided into mishnayos. There are sixty-three masechtos in the Mishna.

SEDER ZERAIM / סֵדֶר זְרָעִים

[ZERAIM = seeds. This section deals with the religious laws pertaining to agriculture.]

Berachos בְּרָכוֹת	Shevi'is שְׁבִיעִית	Challa חַלָּה
Peah פֵּאָה	Terumos תְּרוּמוֹת	Orla עָרְלָה
Demai דְּמַאי	Maasros מַעַשְׂרוֹת	Bikkurim בִּכּוּרִים
Kil'ayim כִּלְאַיִם	Maaser Sheyni מַעֲשֵׂר שֵׁנִי	

SEDER MOED / סֵדֶר מוֹעֵד

[MOED =seasons. This section deals primarily with the laws of the Sabbath and the festivals.]

Shabbat שַׁבָּת	Yoma יוֹמָא	Taanit תַּעֲנִית
Eyruvin עֵרוּבִין	Sukka סֻכָּה	Megilla מְגִלָּה
Pesachim פְּסָחִים	Beytza בֵּיצָה	Moed Katan מוֹעֵד קָטָן
Shekalim שְׁקָלִים	Rosh Hashana רֹאשׁ הַשָּׁנָה	Chagiga חֲגִיגָה

SEDER NASHIM / סֵדֶר נָשִׁים

[NASHIM = women. This section deals with the laws of marriage, divorce and vows.]

Yavamos יְבָמוֹת	Nazir נָזִיר	Sotah סוֹטָה
Kesubos כְּתֻבּוֹת		Gittin גִּטִּין
Nedarim נְדָרִים		Kiddushin קִדּוּשִׁין

SEDER NEZIKIN / סֵדֶר נְזִיקִין

[NEZIKIM = damages. Deals with civil and criminal law.]

Bava Kamma בָּבָא קַמָּא	Makkos מַכּוֹת	Eyduyos עֵדֻיוֹת
Bava Metzia בָּבָא מְצִיעָא	Shevuos שְׁבוּעוֹת	Avoda Zara עֲבוֹדָה זָרָה
Bava Basra בָּבָא בַּתְרָא		Avos אָבוֹת
Sanhedrin סַנְהֶדְרִין		Horayos הוֹרָיוֹת

SEDER KODOSHIM / סֵדֶר קָדָשִׁים

[KODOSHIM = sanctified objects. This section deals with the laws of ritual slaughter, kashrus, sacrifices, and sanctified objects.]

Zevachim זְבָחִים	Arachin עֲרָכִין	Me'ila מְעִילָה
Menachos מְנָחוֹת	Temura תְּמוּרָה	Tamid תָּמִיד
Chullin חֻלִּין	Krisos כְּרִיתוֹת	Middos מִדּוֹת
Bechoros בְּכוֹרוֹת		Kinnim קִנִּים

SEDER TOHOROS / סֵדֶר טָהֳרוֹת

[TOHOROS = purities. Deals with the laws of ceremonial purity.]

Keylim כֵּלִים	Tohoros טָהֳרוֹת	Zavim זָבִים
Ohalos אֲהָלוֹת	Mikvaos מִקְוָאוֹת	Tevul Yom טְבוּל יוֹם
Negaim נְגָעִים	Nidda נִדָּה	Yadayim יָדַיִם
Para פָּרָה	Machshirin מַכְשִׁירִין	Okatzin עֻקְצִין

C/4. The Talmud (Gemarra)

The completion of the Mishna marked the end of the period of the Tannaim and the beginning of the Amoraim. The Amoraim were active in two main centers — Eretz Yisrael and Bavel (Babylonia).

Many generations of Amoraim were involved in explaining and clarifying the masechtos of the Mishna. These explanations of the Amoraim are called the Talmud or the Gemarra.

The Amoraim who lived in Eretz Yisrael produced the Talmud Yerushalmi, and those who lived in Bavel produced the Talmud Bavli. The Talmud Yerushalmi deals with thirty-nine of the sixty-three masechtos of the Mishna; the Talmud Bavli deals with thirty-seven.

	TALMUD BAVLI	TALMUD YERUSHALMI
SEDER ZERAIM		
Berachos	√	√
Peah	—	√
Demai	—	√
Kil'ayim	—	√
Shevi'is	—	√
Terumos	—	√
Maasaros	—	√
Maaser Sheyni	—	√
Challa	—	√
Orla	—	√
Bikkurim	—	√
SEDER MOED		
Shabbos	√	√
Eyruvin	√	√
Pesachim	√	√
Shekalim	—	√
Yoma	√	√
Sukka	√	√
Beytza	√	√
Rosh Hashana	√	√
Taanis	√	√
Megilla	√	√
Moed Katan	√	√
Chagiga	√	√

	TALMUD BAVLI	TALMUD YERUSHALMI
SEDER NASHIM		
Yevamos	√	√
Kesuvos	√	√
Nedarim	√	√
Nazir	√	√
Sotah	√	√
Gittin	√	√
Kiddushin	√	√
SEDER NEZIKIN		
Bava Kamma	√	√
Bava Metzia	√	√
Bava Basra	√	√
Sanhedrin	√	√
Makkos	√	√
Shevuos	√	√
Eyduyos	—	—
Avoda Zara	√	√
Avos	—	—
Horayos	√	√
SEDER KODOSHIM		
Zevachim	√	—
Menachos	√	—
Chullin	√	—
Bechoros	√	—
Arachin	√	—
Temura	√	—
Krisos	√	—
Me'ila	√	—
Tamid	√	—
Middos	—	—
Kinnim	—	—
SEDER TOHOROS		
Keylim	—	—
Oholos	—	—
Negaim	—	—
Para	—	—
Tohoros	—	—
Mikvaos	—	—
Nidda	√	√
Machshirin	—	—
Zavim	—	—
Tevul Yom	—	—
Yadayim	—	—
Okatzin	—	—

C/5. Rambam: Mishneh Torah (Hayad Hachazaka)

This is the Rambam's summary of all the laws in the Torah Sheb'al Peh — the Oral Law. It is divided into fourteen sections:

1. Madda
   מַדָּע

2. Ahava
   אַהֲבָה

3. Zemanim
   זְמַנִּים

4. Nashim
   נָשִׁים

5. Kedusha
   קְדֻשָּׁה

6. Hafla'a
   הַפְלָאָה

7. Zeraim
   זְרָעִים

8. Avoda
   עֲבוֹדָה

9. Korbanos
   קָרְבָּנוֹת

10. Tohora
    טָהֳרָה

11. Nezikin
    נְזִיקִין

12. Kinyan
    קִנְיָן

13. Mishpatim
    מִשְׁפָּטִים

14. Shoftim
    שׁוֹפְטִים

C/6. Shulchan Aruch —
The Code of Jewish Law

The Shulchan Aruch is the authoritative code of law compiled by Rav Yosef Karo and Rav Moshe Isserles in the 1500s. It is divided into four sections:

Orach Chayim
אֹרַח חַיִּים

deals with daily conduct, prayers, Shabbos and festivals

Yoreh Deah
יוֹרֶה דֵּעָה

deals with the dietary laws and other matters

Even Ha'eyzer
אֶבֶן הָעֵזֶר

deals with personal and family matters

Choshen Mishpat
חֹשֶׁן מִשְׁפָּט

deals with civil law and administration

D The Mishkan and the Beis Hamikdash — The Tabernacle and the Holy Temple

D/1. Locations of the Mishkan in Eretz Yisrael

For most of the 479 years from the time the Jews left Egypt until the First Beis Hamikdash was built, the Aron Hakodesh — the Holy Ark — was kept in the Mishkan. The Mishkan was a temporary dwelling place for the Shechina — God's Holy Presence — until the Beis Hamikdash was built. It was first erected in the year 2449. Then it was taken down and carried by the Leviim through the desert for thirty-nine years. When the Jews reached Eretz Yisrael, it stood in the following places:

		(In the desert 39 years)
Gilgal	from 2488	for 14 years
Shilo	from 2503	for 369 years
Nov	from 2871	for 13 years
Giveon	from 2884	for 44 years

Entire period of the Mishkan	= 479 years

The dedication of the First Beis Hamikdash took place in the year 2928.

D/2. Kley Hamishkan — Utensils of the Mishkan

Aron אָרוֹן	The Ark. Also called Aron Ha'edus, Aron Hashem, Aron Habris, Aron HaElokim. Made of acacia wood and covered with gold, the Aron housed the Luchos Habris, the two stone tablets of the Ten Commandments. The Kapores was a sheet of pure gold which covered the open top of the Aron. Atop the Kapores and formed from the same piece of gold, were the two Keruvim, winged figures.
Shulchan שֻׁלְחָן	A gold-covered table for the Lechem Hapanim, the twelve showbreads
Menoras Hamaor מְנוֹרַת הַמָּאוֹר	The gold menora
Mizbach Haketores מִזְבַּח הַקְּטֹרֶת	The gold-covered altar for the ketores, the incense
Mizbach Ha'ola מִזְבַּח הָעוֹלָה	The copper-covered altar for the other sacrifices
Kiyor V'chano כִּיּוֹר וְכַנּוֹ	The copper basin and stand for the priests to wash their hands and feet

D/3. Bigdey Kehuna — the Priests' Clothing

Kohen Gadol - the High Priest

Eyfod אֵפוֹד	An apron-like garment going down the front and back
Choshen חֹשֶׁן	A square of fabric worn on the chest, containing twelve precious stones inscribed with the names of the twelve tribes
Me'il מְעִיל	A long, blue, sleeveless robe with golden pomegranates and bells on the bottom hem
Kutones כְּתֹנֶת	A woven tunic
Mitznefes מִצְנֶפֶת	A turban
Avnet אַבְנֵט	A belt
Tzitz צִיץ	A golden band worn on the forehead with the words "Kodesh Lashem" written on it
Michnasayim מִכְנָסַיִם	Pants

Kohen Hedyot - a regular Priest

Kutones כְּתֹנֶת	A woven tunic
Michnasayim מִכְנָסַיִם	Pants
Migba'as (hat) מִגְבַּעַת	A hat
Avnet אַבְנֵט	A belt

D/4. Korbanos — Sacrifices

KODSHEY KODOSHIM
קָדְשֵׁי קָדָשִׁים

obligatory offering חוֹבָה	obligatory or freewill offering חוֹבָה אוֹ נְדָבָה
chattas חַטָּאת	olah עוֹלָה
asham אָשָׁם	mincha מִנְחָה
shalmey tzibur שַׁלְמֵי צִבּוּר	

KODOSHIM KALIM
קָדָשִׁים קַלִּים

obligatory offering חוֹבָה	obligatory or freewill offering חוֹבָה אוֹ נְדָבָה
bechor בְּכוֹר	shalmey yachid שַׁלְמֵי יָחִיד
ma'sar beheyma מַעְשַׂר בְּהֵמָה	todah תּוֹדָה
pesach פֶּסַח	

E Eretz Yisrael — The Land of Israel

1. GEOGRAPHICAL SECTIONS OF ERETZ YISRAEL

2. SEAS, RIVERS AND MOUNTAINS

3. THE SEVEN NATIONS OF CANAAN

4. OREY MIKLAT — THE SIX CITIES OF REFUGE
   IN ERETZ YISRAEL

5. ANCIENT AND MODERN CITIES IN ERETZ YISRAEL

6. WHERE THE SANHEDRIN MET

7. SHIV'AS HAMINIM — THE SEVEN SPECIES

E

E/1. Geographical Sections of Eretz Yisrael

Shefeyla שְׁפֵלָה	the coastal strip
Har הַר	the mountainous central portion of the country; includes Yehuda (Judea) and Shomron (Samaria)
Negev נֶגֶב	the dry, southern desert; also called the Arava
Bik'a בִּקְעָה	the deep rift to the east of the mountains
Golan גּוֹלָן	the high mountains and plateau in the northeast
Galil גָּלִיל	the northern section of the country
Eyver Hayarden עֵבֶר הַיַּרְדֵּן	the land on the eastern side of the Jordan River

E/2. Seas, Rivers and Mountains

Seas and Rivers

Mediterranean Sea	Hayam Hatichon or Hayam Hagadol הַיָּם הַתִּיכוֹן (הַיָּם הַגָּדוֹל)
Dead Sea	Yam Hamelach יָם הַמֶּלַח
Kinneres or Sea of Galilee	Yam Kinneres יָם כִּנֶּרֶת
Jordan River	Yarden הַיַּרְדֵּן

Israel is a land which is greatly dependent on rain as a source of water. There are many *nechalim* — riverbeds — in Eretz Yisrael, and some of them have water all year long; but many others have water only during the rainy winter season. The Yarden is the longest river in the country.

Mountains

The following is a list of the main mountain ranges, plus several famous individual mountains, from the north of the country to the south.

Har = Mount (singular) = הַר
Harey = the mountains of... (plural) = הָרֵי

Har Chermon	הַר חֶרְמוֹן
Harey Hagolan	הָרֵי הַגּוֹלָן
Har Hacarmel	הַר הַכַּרְמֶל
Harey Shomron	הָרֵי שֹׁמְרוֹן
Harey Hagalil	הָרֵי הַגָּלִיל
Har Miron	הַר מֵירוֹן
Har Hagilboa	הַר הַגִּלְבֹּעַ
Har Tavor	הַר תָּבוֹר
Harey Yehuda	הָרֵי יְהוּדָה
Har Hamoriya (Har Habayis-הַר הַבַּיִת) הַר הַמּוֹרִיָּה
Harey Chevron	הָרֵי חֶבְרוֹן
Harey Moav	הָרֵי מוֹאָב
Harey Edom	הָרֵי אֱדוֹם
Harey Hanegev	הָרֵי הַנֶּגֶב
Harey Eilat	הָרֵי אֵילַת

E/3. The Seven Nations of Canaan

These are the seven nations whom the Jewish people were commanded to conquer in the Land of Canaan (Israel).

The Canaani	הַכְּנַעֲנִי
The Chitti	הַחִתִּי
The Amori	הָאֱמֹרִי
The Prizi	הַפְּרִזִּי
The Chivi	הַחִוִּי
The Yevusi	הַיְבוּסִי
The Girgashi	הַגִּרְגָּשִׁי

E/4. Orey Miklat — the Six Cities of Refuge in Eretz Yisrael

Kedesh	קֶדֶשׁ
Shechem	שְׁכֶם
Chevron	חֶבְרוֹן
Betzer	בֶּצֶר
Ramos	רָאמוֹת
Golan	גוֹלָן

In addition, the forty-two cities which belonged to the Leviim also served as cities of refuge.

E/5. Ancient and Modern Cities in Eretz Yisrael

The names of the following cities are all given according to the Sefaradit pronunciation used in spoken Hebrew today.
— Ancient cities mentioned in the Tanach are marked "T."
— Ancient cities from *after* the period of the Tanach are marked "A."
— Modern cities are marked "M."

Afula (T,M)	עֲפוּלָה
Akko (T,A,M)	עַכּוֹ
Arad (T,M)	עֲרָד
Ashdod (T,M)	אַשְׁדּוֹד
Ashkelon (T,A,M)	אַשְׁקְלוֹן
Azza (T,A,M)	עַזָּה
Bat Yam (M)	בַּת יָם
Beer Sheva (T,A,M)	בְּאֵר שֶׁבַע
Beit Lechem (T,A,M)	בֵּית לֶחֶם
Beit She'an (T,A,M)	בֵּית שְׁאָן
Beit Shemesh (T,M)	בֵּית שֶׁמֶשׁ
Bnei Brak (T,A,M)	בְּנֵי בְּרַק
Chatzor (T,M)	חָצוֹר
Eilat (T,M)	אֵילַת
Hadera (M)	חֲדֵרָה
Haifa (M)	חֵיפָה
Herzliya (M)	הֶרְצְלִיָּה
Hevron (T,A,M)	חֶבְרוֹן
Kfar Saba (M)	כְּפַר סָבָא
Kiryat Arba (T,M)	קִרְיַת אַרְבַּע
Kiryat Gat (T,M)	קִרְיַת גַּת

Kiryat Shemona (T,M.)	קִרְיַת שְׁמוֹנָה
Kiryat Yearim (T)	קִרְיַת יְעָרִים
Lachish (T,M)	לָכִישׁ
Lod (T,A,M)	לֹד
Meggido (T)	מְגִדּוֹ
Nahariya (M)	נַהֲרִיָּה
Natzeret (A,M)	נַצְרֶת
Netanya (M)	נְתַנְיָה
Petach Tikva (M)	פֶּתַח תִּקְוָה
Raanana (M)	רַעֲנַנָּה
Rama (T)	רָמָה
Ramat Gan (M)	רָמַת גַּן
Ramleh (A,M)	רַמְלָה
Rechovot (T,M)	רְחוֹבוֹת
Rishon Lezion (M)	רִאשׁוֹן לְצִיּוֹן
Sedom (T,M)	סְדוֹם
Shechem (T,A,M)	שְׁכֶם
Shiloh (T)	שִׁילֹה
Tel Aviv (M)	תֵּל־אָבִיב
Teverya (A,M)	טְבֶרְיָה
Tzefat (A,M)	צְפַת
Yafo (T,A,M)	יָפוֹ
Yericho (T,A,M)	יְרִיחוֹ
Yerushalayim (T,A,M)	יְרוּשָׁלַיִם
Zichron Yaakov (M)	זִכְרוֹן יַעֲקֹב

E/6. Where the Sanhedrin Met

The normal meeting place of the Sanhedrin (the High Court) was in the Lishkas Hagazis, one of the chambers in the Beis Hamikdash. After the destruction of the Second Temple, the Sanhedrin was no longer able to meet in Jerusalem. Instead, during different periods, the Sanhedrin met in the following places

Yavneh	יַבְנֶה
Usha	אוּשָׁה
Shefaram	שְׁפַרְעָם
Beis Shearim	בֵּית שְׁעָרִים
Tzippori	צִפּוֹרִי
Teverya	טְבֶרְיָה

E/7. Shiv'as Haminim — the Seven Species

The seven types of plants with which the Land of Israel was especially blessed.

Wheat	chitta	חִטָּה
Barley	se'ora	שְׂעוֹרָה
Grapes	gefen	גֶּפֶן
Figs	t'ayna	תְּאֵנָה
Pomegranates	rimon	רִמּוֹן
Olives	zeis shemen	זֵית שֶׁמֶן
Dates *	devash	דְּבַשׁ

* In Biblical terminology, "devash" always refers to dates, although in modern Hebrew usage it means "honey."

F All in Hebrew: Lashon Hakodesh — the Holy Language

F

F/1. Alef-Beis: the Alphabet and the Vowels

		NUMERICAL VALUE
alef	א	1
beis/veis	בּ, ב	2
gimmel	ג	3
dales	ד	4
hey	ה	5
vav	ו	6
zayin	ז	7
ches	ח	8
tes	ט	9
yod	י	10
kaf/chaf	כּ, כ, ך	20
lamed	ל	30
mem	מ, ם	40
nun	נ, ן	50
samech	ס	60
ayin	ע	70
pey/fey	פּ, פ, ף	80
tzadi	צ, ץ	90
kof	ק	100
reysh	ר	200
shin/sin	שׁ, שׂ	300
tav/sav	תּ, ת	400

THE VOWELS

kamatz	ָ	קָמַץ
patach	ַ	פַּתָח
tzeyreh	ֵי ֵ	צֵירֶה
segol	ֶ	סֶגוֹל
chirik	ִי ִ	חִירִיק
cholam	וֹ ֹ	חוֹלָם
shuruk	וּ	שׁוּרוּק
kubutz	ֻ	קֻבּוּץ
chataf patach	ֲ	חֲטַף פַּתָח
chataf segol	ֱ	חֲטַף סֶגוֹל
chataf kamatz	ֳ	חֲטַף קָמַץ
sh'va	ְ	שְׁוָא

F/2. Numbers

	masc. form	fem. form
one	echod אֶחָד	achas אַחַת
two	shenayim שְׁנַיִם	shetayim שְׁתַּיִם
three	shelosha שְׁלֹשָׁה	shalosh שָׁלֹשׁ
four	arba'a אַרְבָּעָה	arba אַרְבַּע
five	chamisha חֲמִשָּׁה	chamesh חָמֵשׁ
six	shisha שִׁשָּׁה	shesh שֵׁשׁ
seven	shiv'a שִׁבְעָה	sheva שֶׁבַע
eight	shemona שְׁמוֹנָה	shemoneh שְׁמוֹנֶה
nine	tish'a תִּשְׁעָה	teysha תֵּשַׁע
ten	asara עֲשָׂרָה	eser עֶשֶׂר
eleven	achad asar אַחַד־עָשָׂר	achas esrey אַחַת־עֶשְׂרֵה
twelve	shneym asar שְׁנֵים־עָשָׂר	shteym esrey שְׁתֵּים־עֶשְׂרֵה
thirteen	shelosha asar שְׁלֹשָׁה־עָשָׂר	shelosh esrey שְׁלֹשׁ־עֶשְׂרֵה
fourteen	arba'a asar אַרְבָּעָה־עָשָׂר	arba esrey אַרְבַּע־עֶשְׂרֵה
fifteen	chamisha asar חֲמִשָּׁה־עָשָׂר	chamesh esrey חֲמֵשׁ־עֶשְׂרֵה
sixteen	shisha asar שִׁשָּׁה־עָשָׂר	shesh esrey שֵׁשׁ־עֶשְׂרֵה
seventeen	shiv'a asar שִׁבְעָה־עָשָׂר	sheva esrey שְׁבַע־עֶשְׂרֵה
eighteen	shemona asar שְׁמוֹנָה־עָשָׂר	shemoneh esrey שְׁמוֹנֶה־עֶשְׂרֵה

nineteen	tish'a asar תִּשְׁעָה־עָשָׂר	tesha esrey תְּשַׁע־עֶשְׂרֵה
twenty	esrim עֶשְׂרִים	
thirty	sheloshim שְׁלֹשִׁים	
forty	arba'im אַרְבָּעִים	
fifty	chamishim חֲמִשִּׁים	
sixty	shishim שִׁשִּׁים	
seventy	shiv'im שִׁבְעִים	
eighty	shemonim שְׁמוֹנִים	
ninety	tish'im תִּשְׁעִים	
one hundred	meya מֵאָה	
one thousand	elef אֶלֶף	
ten thousand	ribo רִבּוֹא	

F/3. Directions

North	tzafon	צָפוֹן
South	darom	דָּרוֹם
East	mizrach	מִזְרָח
West	ma'arav	מַעֲרָב

F/4. The Heavens

sun	shemesh, chamma	שֶׁמֶשׁ, חַמָּה
moon	levana, yareyach	לְבָנָה, יָרֵחַ
star	kochav	כּוֹכָב

The Planets

Mercury	Kochav	כּוֹכָב
Venus	Nogah	נֹגַהּ
Earth	Eretz	אֶרֶץ
Mars	Ma'adim	מַאְדִּים
Jupiter	Tzedek	צֶדֶק
Saturn	Shabsai	שַׁבְּתַאי
Uranus	Uranus	אוּרָנוּס
Neptune	Neptune	נֶפְּטוּן
Pluto	Pluto	פְּלוּטוֹ

The Zodiac

Lamb	Taleh	טָלֶה
Ox	Shor	שׁוֹר
Twins	Teomim	תְּאוֹמִים
Crab	Sartan	סַרְטָן
Lion	Aryeh	אַרְיֵה
Maiden	Besula	בְּתוּלָה
Scales	Moznayim	מֹאזְנַיִם
Scorpion	Akrav	עַקְרָב
Bow	Keshes	קֶשֶׁת
Kid	Gedi	גְּדִי
Bucket	Deli	דְּלִי
Fish	Dagim	דָּגִים

F/5. Geography and Weather

Geography

continent	yabeshes	יַבֶּשֶׁת
land	adama	אֲדָמָה
country	eretz	אֶרֶץ
state	medina	מְדִינָה
mountain	har	הַר
hill	giv'a	גִּבְעָה
water	mayim	מַיִם
ocean	yam	יָם
river	nahar	נָהָר
stream	nachal	נַחַל
spring	ma'ayan	מַעְיָן
well	b'ehr	בְּאֵר

Seasons

winter	choref	חֹרֶף
spring	aviv	אָבִיב
summer	kayitz	קַיִץ
fall	sesav	סְתָו

Weather

rain	geshem	גֶּשֶׁם
	matar	מָטָר
	yoreh (first rains of season)	יוֹרֶה
	malkosh (last rains)	מַלְקוֹשׁ
dew	tal	טַל
snow	sheleg	שֶׁלֶג
ice	kerach	קֶרַח
wind	ruach	רוּחַ
storm	se'ara	סְעָרָה
lightning	barak	בָּרָק
thunder	ra'am	רַעַם
heat	chom	חֹם
cold	kor	קֹר

General

sand	chol	חוֹל
dust	avak	אָבָק

F/6. Something about Plants

tree	eytz	עֵץ
trunk	geza	גֶּזַע
root	shoresh	שֹׁרֶשׁ
flower	perach	פֶּרַח
bud	nitzan	נִצָּן
leaf	aleh	עָלֶה
bush	si'ach	שִׂיחַ
produce (grains)	tevua	תְּבוּאָה
fruit	pri, peyros	פְּרִי, פֵּרוֹת
vegetables	yerakos	יְרָקוֹת

F/7. Colors

red	adom	אָדֹם
black	shachor	שָׁחֹר
blue	kachol	כָּחֹל
green	yarok	יָרֹק
yellow	tzahov	צָהֹב
brown	chum	חוּם
purple	sagol	סָגֹל
orange	kasom	כָּתֹם
gold	zahov	זָהֹב
silver	kasof	כָּסֹף
gray	afor	אָפֹר
white	lavan	לָבָן
light blue	techeles	תְּכֵלֶת

F/8. Parts of the Body

skull	gulgoles	גֻּלְגֹּלֶת
head	rosh	רֹאשׁ
eye	ayin	עַיִן
ear	ozen	אֹזֶן
nose	af	אַף
jaw	leses	לֶסֶת
mouth	peh	פֶּה
tongue	lashon	לָשׁוֹן
teeth	shinayim	שִׁנַּיִם
chin	santer	סַנְטֵר
cheek	lechi	לְחִי
neck	tzavar	צַוָּאר
throat	garon	גָּרוֹן
shoulder	kasef	כָּתֵף
chest	chazeh	חָזֶה
stomach	beten	בֶּטֶן
back	gav	גַּב
hand	yad	יָד
arm	zeroa	זְרוֹעַ
elbow	marpek	מַרְפֵּק
finger	etzba	אֶצְבַּע
thumb	agudal	אֲגוּדָל
hip	yarech	יָרֵךְ
foot	regel	רֶגֶל
knee	berech	בֶּרֶךְ
ankle	karsol	קַרְסֹל
heel	akev	עָקֵב
bone	etzem	עֶצֶם
heart	lev	לֵב
lung	reya	רֵאָה
kidney	kilya	כִּלְיָה
blood	dahm	דָּם

F/9. People, Family and Friends

family	mishpacha	מִשְׁפָּחָה
friend	chaver	חָבֵר
	rey'a, yadid	רֵעַ, יָדִיד
Mr.	adon, mar	אָדוֹן, מַר
Mrs.	geveres	גְּבֶרֶת
man	ish	אִישׁ
woman	isha	אִשָּׁה
baby	tinok	תִּינוֹק
boy	yeled	יֶלֶד
	na'ar, bachur	נַעַר, בָּחוּר
girl	yalda	יַלְדָּה
	na'ara, bachura	נַעֲרָה, בַּחוּרָה
husband	ba'al	בַּעַל
wife	isha	אִשָּׁה
father	av (abba)	אָב (אַבָּא)
mother	aym (imma)	אֵם (אִמָּא)
brother	ach	אָח
sister	achos	אָחוֹת
grandfather	sav (sabba)	סָב (סַבָּא)
grandmother	sava (savta)	סָבָה (סַבְתָּא)
grandson	neched	נֶכֶד
granddaughter	nechda	נֶכְדָּה
uncle	dod	דּוֹד
aunt	doda	דּוֹדָה
nephew	achyan	אַחְיָן
niece	achyanis	אַחְיָנִית
cousin (boy)	ben-dod	בֶּן-דּוֹד
cousin (girl)	bas-doda	בַּת-דּוֹדָה
father-in-law	cham, chosen	חָם, חוֹתֵן
mother-in-law	chamos, chosenes	חָמוֹת, חוֹתֶנֶת
son-in-law	chasan	חָתָן
daughter-in-law	kalla	כַּלָּה
brother-in-law	gees	גִּיס
sister-in-law	geesa	גִּיסָה

G Berachos — Blessings

There are many blessings which a Jew recites during his lifetime — blessings upon a marriage, for a circumcision, for the redemption of the firstborn son; for redeeming one's vineyard in the fourth year, for going to the cemetery for the first time in thirty days, and, of course, for all the other mitzvos one performs — putting on tefillin, lighting the Sabbath candles, etc. The following is a listing of the many blessings we recite over things we eat, smell, see, and hear. It is not meant to be a guide. If you have any questions about which blessing to say, ask a parent or teacher or someone else who knows the exact halacha. Most berachos are recited *before* performing the activity.

All blessings start with the words:

בָּרוּךְ אַתָּה ה׳, אֱלֹקֵינוּ, מֶלֶךְ הָעוֹלָם,
Blessed are You, Hashem, our God, King of the universe,

Then, depending on the particular blessing, we add:

G/1. For Things We Eat

Bread

‎...הַמּוֹצִיא לֶחֶם מִן הָאָרֶץ.

...hamotzi lechem min ha'aretz.

...Who brings forth bread from the earth.

Cake or food made or baked from the five grains: wheat, barley, rye, oats, spelt

‎...בּוֹרֵא מִינֵי מְזוֹנוֹת.

...borey miney mezonos.

...Who creates all types of nourishment.

Wine or grape juice

‎...בּוֹרֵא פְּרִי הַגָּפֶן.

...borey pri hagafen.

...Who creates the fruit of the wine.

Fruit from a tree

‎...בּוֹרֵא פְּרִי הָעֵץ.

...borey pri ha'eytz.

...Who creates the fruit of the tree.

Vegetables or things which are newly planted each year

‎...בּוֹרֵא פְּרִי הָאֲדָמָה.

...borey pri ha'adama.

...Who creates the fruit of the ground.

Liquids, eggs, fish, meat & other foods

‎...שֶׁהַכֹּל נִהְיָה בִּדְבָרוֹ.

...shehakol nih'ya bidevaro.

...through Whose word everything came into being.

G/2. After We Eat

Birkas Hamazon
We say the blessing *Birkas Hamazon* after eating
a meal with bread.

Al Hamichya
We say the blessing *Al Hamichya* after eating
cake or mezonos food.

Al Hagefen
We say the blessing *Al Hagefen* after drinking
wine or grape juice.

Al Ha'eytz
We say the blessing *Al Ha'eytz* after eating any of
the Seven Species of plants (see section E/7):
Wheat and Barley (except when they are baked as
bread or matzah), Grapes (or wine), Figs,
Pomegranates, Olives and Dates.

Borey Nefashos
We say the blessing *Borey Nefashos* after eating
other foods.

G/3. For Things We Smell

Fragrant spices

...בּוֹרֵא מִינֵי בְשָׂמִים.

...borey miney vesamim.

...Who creates different types of spices.

Fragrant plants

...בּוֹרֵא עִשְׂבֵי בְשָׂמִים.

...borey isvay vesamim.

...Who creates fragrant plants.

Spice trees

...בּוֹרֵא עֲצֵי בְשָׂמִים.

...borey atzey vesamim.

...Who creates fragrant spice trees.

Fragrant fruits

...הַנּוֹתֵן רֵיחַ טוֹב בַּפֵּרוֹת.

...hanosen reyach tov bapeyros.

...Who gives a pleasant aroma to fruits.

G/4. For Things We See

Lightning, falling stars, exceptionally high mountains or great deserts

...עוֹשֶׂה מַעֲשֵׂה בְרֵאשִׁית.

...oseh ma'aseh vereyshit.

...Who sustains the act of creation.

An Ocean

...שֶׁעָשָׂה אֶת הַיָּם הַגָּדוֹל.

...she'asa es hayam hagadol.

...Who made the great sea.

A rainbow

...זוֹכֵר הַבְּרִית וְנֶאֱמָן בִּבְרִיתוֹ וְקַיָּם בְּמַאֲמָרוֹ.

...zocher habris vene'eman bivriso v'kayam bema'amaro.

...Who remembers the Covenant, is faithful to His Covenant, and Who fulfills His Word.

Very beautiful trees or animals

...שֶׁכָּכָה לוֹ בְּעוֹלָמוֹ.

...shekacha lo be'olamo.

...Who has these in His world.

Fruit trees blossoming for the first time that year

...שֶׁלֹּא חִסַּר בְּעוֹלָמוֹ דָּבָר וּבָרָא בוֹ בְּרִיּוֹת טוֹבוֹת וְאִילָנוֹת טוֹבִים לְהַנּוֹת בָּהֶם בְּנֵי אָדָם.

...shelo chisar be'olamo davar, uvarah vo beriyos tovos v'ilanos tovim lehanos bahem b'nei adam.

...Who has left nothing lacking in His world, and has created in it pleasant creatures and good trees to give pleasure to mankind.

Upon seeing a great Torah scholar

...שֶׁחָלַק מֵחָכְמָתוֹ לִירֵאָיו.

...shechalak meychochmaso lireyav.

...Who has imparted of His wisdom to those that revere Him.

continued on next page

**Upon seeing a great scholar or wise man
who is a non-Jew**

שֶׁנָּתַן מֵחָכְמָתוֹ לְבָשָׂר וָדָם...

...shenasan meychochmaso levasar vadam.

...Who has given of His wisdom to mortal men.

Upon seeing 600,000 Jews all together

חֲכַם הָרָזִים...

...chacham harazim.

...He Who understands the secret thoughts of all men.

**Upon seeing unusually formed people or animals,
such as giants or dwarfs**

מְשַׁנֶּה הַבְּרִיּוֹת...

...meshaneh haberiyos.

...Who changes the forms of creatures.

**Upon seeing a place where a great miracle was
performed**

שֶׁעָשָׂה נֵס לַאֲבוֹתֵינוּ בַּמָּקוֹם הַזֶּה...

...she asa nes la'avoseynu bamakom hazeh.

...Who performed a miracle for our fathers in this place.

or

שֶׁעָשָׂה לִי נֵס בַּמָּקוֹם הַזֶּה...

...she'asa li nes bamakom hazeh.

...Who performed a miracle for me in this place.

G/5. For Things We Hear

Thunder

...שֶׁכֹּחוֹ וּגְבוּרָתוֹ מָלֵא עוֹלָם.

...shekocho ugevuraso maley olam.

...Whose strength and might fill the world.

On hearing good news

...הַטּוֹב וְהַמֵּטִיב.

...hatov vehameytiv.

...Who is good and Who does good for others.

On hearing bad news

...דַּיַּן הָאֱמֶת.

...dayan ha'emes.

...the true Judge.

G/6. Other Blessings

When doing a mitzva or eating fruits for the first time in a new season, or when wearing new clothing, we recite the blessing

...שֶׁהֶחֱיָנוּ וְקִיְּמָנוּ וְהִגִּיעָנוּ לַזְּמַן הַזֶּה.

...shehecheyanu vekiyemanu vehigianu lazman hazeh.

...Who has kept us alive, and has preserved us, and has brought us to this season.

continued on next page

For putting up a fence around a roof or a large hole

אֲשֶׁר קִדְּשָׁנוּ בְּמִצְוֹתָיו וְצִוָּנוּ לַעֲשׂוֹת מַעֲקֶה.

...asher kideshanu bemitzvosav vetzivanu la'asos ma'akeh.

...Who has sanctified us with His commandments and commanded us to erect a barrier.

For putting up a mezuza

אֲשֶׁר קִדְּשָׁנוּ בְּמִצְוֹתָיו וְצִוָּנוּ לִקְבֹּעַ מְזוּזָה.

...asher kideshanu bemitzvosav vetzivanu likboa mezuza.

...Who has sanctified us with His commandments and commanded us to put up a mezuza.

For immersing dishes in the mikva

אֲשֶׁר קִדְּשָׁנוּ בְּמִצְוֹתָיו וְצִוָּנוּ עַל טְבִילַת כֵּלִים.

...asher kideshanu bemitzvosav vetzivanu al tevilas keylim.

...Who has sanctified us with His commandments and commanded us concerning the immersion of utensils.

For separating "challah" from dough

אֲשֶׁר קִדְּשָׁנוּ בְּמִצְוֹתָיו וְצִוָּנוּ לְהַפְרִישׁ חַלָּה מִן הָעִסָּה.

...asher kideshanu bemitzvosav vetzivanu lehafrish challah min ha'isa.

...Who has sanctified us with His commandments and commanded us to separate the challah from the dough.

For separating Terumos and Ma'asros (tithing)...

אֲשֶׁר קִדְּשָׁנוּ בְּמִצְוֹתָיו וְצִוָּנוּ לְהַפְרִישׁ תְּרוּמוֹת וּמַעַשְׂרוֹת.

...asher kideshanu bemitzvosav vetzivanu lehafrish terumos uma'asros.

...Who has sanctified us with His commandments and commanded us to separate terumos and ma'asros.

H Time — All Around the Calendar

H

H/1. Periods in Jewish History

NOTE: When using the standard Gregorian calendar, we use the following abbreviations:

B.C.E. = Before the Common Era = before the Gregorian year 1.

C.E. = Common Era = beginning with the Gregorian year 1.

	HEBREW DATES	STANDARD YEAR
Ten generations from Adam to Noach	1-1056	3760-2705 B.C.E.
Ten generations from Noach to Avraham	1056-1948	2705-1813 B.C.E.
Seven generations from Avraham to Moshe	1948-2368	1813-1393 B.C.E.
Moshe to the Judges	2368-2488	1393-1273 B.C.E.
Forty years in the desert	2448-2488	1313-1273 B.C.E.
Period of the Judges	2488-2870	1273-891 B.C.E.
Shmuel the Prophet and Kings David and Shlomo	2871-2964	890-797 B.C.E.
The First Temple	2928-3338	833-423 B.C.E.
The prophets and the kingdoms of Judah and Israel	c.2964-3338	797-423 B.C.E.
The Second Temple	3408-3828	353 B.C.E.-68 C.E.
The Tannaim	c.3450-4000	311 B C.E.-240 C.E.
The Amoraim	c.4000-4260	240-500 C.E.
The Savoraim	c.4260-4450	500-690 C.E.
The Geonim	c.4450-4800	690-1040 C.E.
The Rishonim	c.4800-5200	1040-1440 C.E.
The Acharonim	c.5200	until today

H/2. Important Historical Dates

	HEBREW YEAR	STANDARD YEAR
The Creation of Adam	1	3760 B.C.E.
The Flood	1656	2105 B.C.E.
The Tower of Bavel	1996	1765 B.C.E.
Avraham and the Bris ben Habesarim	2018	1743 B.C.E.
Akeydas Yitzchak	2085	1676 B.C.E.
Yaakov and family go to Egypt	2238	1523 B.C.E.
The Exodus from Egypt	2448	1313 B.C.E.
Receiving the Torah	2448	1313 B.C.E.
Erecting the Mishkan	2449	1312 B.C.E.
Entering Eretz Yisrael	2488	1273 B.C.E.
Start of King David's reign	2854	907 B.C.E.
Destruction of 1st Beis Hamikdash	3338	423 B.C.E.
Miracle of Purim	3405	356 B.C.E.
Miracle of Chanukah	3622	139 B.C.E.
Destruction of 2nd Beis Hamikdash	3828	68 C.E.
Completion of the Mishna	3948	188 C.E.
Completion of the Talmud Yerushalmi	4128	368 C.E.
Completion of the Talmud Bavli	4260	500 C.E.
Birth of Rashi	4800	1040 C.E.
Birth of the Rambam	4894	1134 C.E.
First Expulsion of Jews from France	4946	1186 C.E.

continued on next page

H/2. Important Historical Dates (continued)

	HEBREW YEAR	STANDARD YEAR
The Aliya of 300 Rabbis — Ba'aley Hatosafos — from France and England	4971	1211 C.E.
Burning of the Talmud in France	5011	1251 C.E.
Expulsion from England	5020	1260 C.E.
Beginning of the Inquisition in Spain	5240	1480 C.E.
Birth of Rabi Yosef Karo	5248	1488 C.E.
Expulsion from Spain	5252	1492 C.E.
Birth of HaAri	5294	1534 C.E.
Burning of Talmud in Italy	5314	1554 C.E.
Aliya of the students of the Ba'al Shem Tov	5537	1777 C.E.
Aliya of the students of the Vilna Gaon	5568	1808 C.E.
Beginning of World War I	5674	1914 C.E.
Beginning of World War II	5699	1939 C.E.
Founding of the State of Israel	5708	1948 C.E.
Six-Day War	5727	1967 C.E.

H/3. The Months and their Zodiac signs

Nissan	Taleh (The Lamb)
Iyar	Shor (The Ox)
Sivan	Teomim (The Twins)
Tammuz	Sartan (The Crab)
Av	Aryeh (The Lion)
Elul	Besula (The Maiden)
Tishrey	Moznayim (The Scales)
Cheshvan	Akrav (The Scorpion)
Kislev	Keshes (The Bow)
Teves	Gedi (The Kid)
Shevat	Deli (The Bucket)
Adar	Dagim (The Fish)

H/4. Leap Years

During a leap year, an additional month — Adar Beis — is added to the Jewish calendar. This happens seven times every nineteen years — on the 3rd, 6th, 8th, 11th, 14th, 17th and 19th years in the cycle. Here are three complete leap year cycles.

YEAR IN THE CYCLE	HEBREW YEAR	STANDARD YEAR
3rd	5722	(1961/62)
6th	5725	(1964/65)
8th	5727	(1966/67)
11th	5730	(1969/70)
14th	5733	(1972/73)
17th	5736	(1975/76)
19th	5738	(1977/78)
3rd	5741	(1980/81)
6th	5744	(1983/84)
8th	5746	(1985/86)
11th	5749	(1988/89)
14th	5752	(1991/92)
17th	5755	(1994/95)
19th	5757	(1996/97)
3rd	5760	(1999/2000)
6th	5763	(2002/03)
8th	5765	(2004/05)
11th	5768	(2007/08)
14th	5771	(2010/11)
17th	5774	(2013/14)
19th	5776	(2015/16)

H/5. Shemitta Years

Every seventh year is a shemitta year — a Sabbath year for the Land of Israel, just as every seventh day is the Sabbath day for the Jewish people. In the shemitta year, the Land of Israel is not to be worked; crops are neither planted nor harvested. The following are the shemitta years beginning with the Hebrew year 5712 (1951/52).

HEBREW YEAR	STANDARD YEAR
5712	(1951/52)
5719	(1958/59)
5726	(1965/66)
5733	(1972/73)
5740	(1979/80)
5747	(1986/87)
5754	(1993/94)
5761	(2000/2001)
5768	(2007/2008)
5775	(2014/2015)
5782	(2021/2022)
5789	(2028/2029)
5796	(2035/2023)
5803	(2042/2043)
5810	(2049/2050)

H/6. Birkas Hachamma — Blessing of the Sun

Every twenty-eight years, on a Wednesday morning in the month of Nissan, a cycle comes full term in the heavens. The sun, as seen from the earth, is in the exact location in the sky as it was on the day of its creation. On that day we say Birkas Hachamma — a blessing of thanksgiving and praise to God who "sustains the act of creation."

Birkas Hachamma took place in

HEBREW YEAR	STANDARD YEAR
5685	1925
5713	1953
5741	1981

and will next take place in

5769	2009
5797	2037

H/7. Chagim and Yemay Tzom — Holidays and Fast Days

Holidays

Rosh Hashana	1 & 2 Tishrey
Yom Kippur	10 Tishrey
Sukkos	15 Tishrey
Shemini Atzeres and Simchas Torah in Israel	22 Tishrey
(Shemini Atzeres in other countries	22 Tishrey)
(Simchas Torah in other countries	23 Tishrey)
Chanuka	25 Kislev
Tu B'Shevat	15 Shevat
Purim	14 Adar
Shushan Purim	15 Adar
Pesach	15 Nissan
Lag Ba'Omer	18 Iyar
Shavuos	6 Sivan

Fast Days

Tzom Gedalya	3 Tishrey
Yom Kippur	10 Tishrey
Assara B'Teves	10 Teves
Ta'anis Esther	13 Adar
Shiv'a Assar B'Tammuz	17 Tammuz
Tish'a B'Av	9 Av

H/8. The Four New Years

There are four different beginnings to a Hebrew Year:

ROSH CHODESH NISSAN is the beginning of the year for...
counting the reigns of kings;
counting the months;
counting the Shalosh Regalim — the three
　　annual pilgrimages to Jerusalem.

ROSH CHODESH ELUL is the beginning of the year for ma'sar beheyma — tithing animals.

ROSH CHODESH TISHREY is the beginning of the year for...
counting the calendar years
counting the shemitta years
counting the yovalos (the fiftieth Jubilee years)
n'tiah — the laws of orla and neta reva'i for
　　fruit trees
Rosh Hashana Ladin — God's judging of man.

TU B'SHEVAT — the fifteenth of Shevat — is the beginning of the year for the laws governing the tithing of fruit trees.

H/9. The Four Seasons of the Year

spring	aviv	אָבִיב
summer	kayitz	קַיִץ
fall	sesav	סְתָו
winter	choref	חֹרֶף

H/10. The Four Exiles

Galus Bavel
גָּלוּת בָּבֶל

The Babylonian Exile. After Nevuchadnezzar of Babylonia destroyed the First Temple, the Jews of Israel were sent to Babylonia for seventy years.

Galus Paras U'Madai
גָּלוּת פָּרַס וּמָדַי

The Exile of Persia and Media. The Babylonian Empire was overthrown and the Jews came under the rule of the new conquerers — Persia and Media.

Galus Yavan
גָּלוּת יָוָן

The Greek Exile. During the period of the Second Temple, much of Asia was conquered by the Syrian-Greeks who ruled the Jews as well.

Galus Edom
גָּלוּת אֱדוֹם

The Roman Exile. The destruction of the Second Temple and the complete subjugation of the Jewish people by Rome. The Exile will end with the coming of the Mashiach, the return of all the Jews to the Land of Israel, and the building of the Third Temple — may it take place soon, in our lifetime.

Miscellanea: Middos, Mitzvos, Melachos, Measurements and More...

1. ASSERES HADIBROS — THE TEN COMMANDMENTS

2. SHEVA MITZVOS B'NEI NOACH —
   SEVEN COMMANDMENTS GIVEN TO
   THE DESCENDANTS OF NOACH

3. THIRTY-NINE AV MELACHOS — THE THIRTY-NINE
   PRIMARY ACTIVITIES PROHIBITED ON THE SABBATH

4. THE THIRTEEN ANI MAAMINS — THE THIRTEEN
   PRINCIPLES OF FAITH

5. THIRTEEN MIDDOS (CHARACTER TRAITS) OF
   RABI YISRAEL OF SALANT

6. SHESH ZECHIROS — SIX THINGS TO REMEMBER

7. DAILY AND HOLIDAY PRAYERS

8. MIDDOS — MEASUREMENTS

9. ARBA PARSHIYOS — FOUR SPECIAL TORAH READINGS

10. TEN TRIALS OF AVRAHAM AVINU

11. ESSER MAKKOS — THE TEN PLAGUES

12. ASSARA HARUGEY MALCHUS — THE TEN MARTYRS

I/1. Asseres Hadibros — the Ten Commandments

The following is only an abbreviated listing of the Ten Commandments to help you remember them in the proper order. The full text appears twice in the Torah: Shemos 20:1-14 and Devarim 5:6-18.

1. I am the Lord your God Who took you out of the land of Egypt, from the house of slavery...
   אָנֹכִי ה׳ אֱלֹקֶיךָ אֲשֶׁר הוֹצֵאתִיךָ מֵאֶרֶץ מִצְרַיִם מִבֵּית עֲבָדִים.

2. You shall have no other gods before Me...
   לֹא יִהְיֶה לְךָ אֱלֹהִים אֲחֵרִים עַל פָּנָי...

3. You shall not use the name of the Lord your God in vain...
   לֹא תִשָּׂא אֶת שֵׁם ה׳ אֱלֹקֶיךָ לַשָּׁוְא...

4. Remember the Sabbath day to keep it holy...
   זָכוֹר אֶת יוֹם הַשַּׁבָּת לְקַדְּשׁוֹ...

5. Honor your father and mother...
   כַּבֵּד אֶת אָבִיךָ וְאֶת אִמֶּךָ...

6. You shall not kill.
   לֹא תִרְצָח.

7. You shall not commit adultery.
   לֹא תִנְאָף.

8. You shall not steal.
   לֹא תִגְנֹב.

9. You shall not bear false witness against your neighbor.
   לֹא תַעֲנֶה בְרֵעֲךָ עֵד שָׁקֶר.

10. You shall not covet...
    לֹא תַחְמֹד...

I/2. Sheva Mitzvos B'nei Noach — seven commandments given to the descendants of Noach

All people, Jews and Gentiles alike, were commanded by God to refrain from committing the following six sins; and all were instructed to fulfill the seventh commandment.

DO NOT

1. Worship idols

2. Murder

3. Steal

4. Eat the limbs of animals which are still alive

5. Curse God

6. Commit adultery

DO

7. Appoint judges and set up courts of justice

I/3. Thirty-nine Av Melachos — the thirty-nine primary activities prohibited on the Sabbath

These thirty-nine types of activities were all necessary for the building of the Mishkan. They encompass all possible areas of creative, human "labor" and they serve as the thirty-nine main types of activities which are forbidden on the Sabbath.

1.	Plowing	חֲרִישָׁה
2.	Sowing	זְרִיעָה
3.	Reaping	קְצִירָה
4.	Sheaf-making	עִמּוּר
5.	Threshing	דִּישָׁה
6.	Winnowing	זְרִיָּה
7.	Selecting	בְּרֵרָה
8.	Grinding	טְחִינָה
9.	Sifting	הַרְקָדָה
10.	Kneading	לִישָׁה
11.	Baking	אֲפִיָּה
12.	Sheep-shearing	גְּזִיזָה
13.	Bleaching	לִבּוּן
14.	Combing	נִפּוּץ
15.	Dyeing	צְבִיעָה
16.	Spinning	טְוִיָּה
17.		עֲשִׂיַּת בָּתֵּי נִירִין
18.	nos. 17-20 are all parts of the	הֲסָכַת הַמַּסֶּכֶת
19.	weaving process	אֲרִיגָה
20.		פְּצִיעָה
21.	Tying a knot	קְשִׁירָה

continued on next page

22.	Untying a knot	הַתָּרָה
23.	Sewing	תְּפִירָה
24.	Tearing	קְרִיעָה
25.	Trapping	צִידָה
26.	Slaughtering	שְׁחִיטָה
27.	Skinning	הַפְשָׁטַת הָעוֹר
28.	Tanning	עִבּוּד הָעוֹר
29.	Scraping	מְחִיקַת הָעוֹר
30.	Marking	שִׂרְטוּט
31.	Cutting to size or shape	חִתּוּךְ
32.	Writing	כְּתִיבָה
33.	Erasing	מְחִיקָה
34.	Building	בְּנִיָּה
35.	Demolishing	סְתִירָה
36.	Extinguishing a fire	כִּבּוּי
37.	Kindling a fire	הַבְעָרָה
38.	"Final hammer-blow" (completing an activity)	הַכָּאָה בְּפַטִּישׁ
39.	Removing things from one type of area to another	הוֹצָאָה מֵרְשׁוּת לִרְשׁוּת

I/4. The Thirteen Ani-Maamins — the Thirteen Principles of Faith

The following Thirteen Principles were defined by the Rambam and are recited by many people every morning after the Shacharis prayers.

אֲנִי מַאֲמִין בֶּאֱמוּנָה שְׁלֵמָה
I believe with complete faith...

...that the Creator, blessed is His Name, creates and guides all creatures, and that He alone made, makes, and will make everything.

...that the Creator, blessed is His Name, is absolutely unique and that there is nothing else like Him and that He alone is our God Who was, is and always will be.

...that the Creator, blessed is His Name, is not a physical being, that nothing physical can ever affect Him, and that there is nothing in the world which is comparable to Him.

...that the Creator, blessed is His Name, is the first and the last.

...that to the Creator, blessed is His Name, and to Him alone, it is proper to pray, and it is not proper to pray to anyone else besides Him.

...that the words of all the prophets are true.

...that the prophecy of Moses our Teacher, may peace be upon him, was true, and that he was the father of all prophets, those who came before him, and those who came after.

...that the entire Torah which is now in our hands is the same Torah which was given to Moses our Teacher, may peace be upon him.

continued on next page

...that this Torah will not be exchanged, nor will there ever be another Torah from the Creator, blessed is His Name.

...that the Creator, blessed is His Name, knows all the deeds of men and all their thoughts, as it is said, "It is He Who fashions the hearts of them all together; it is He Who understands their deeds."

...that the Creator, blessed is His Name, rewards those who keep His commandments and punishes those who violate His commandments.

...in the coming of the Mashiach, and even though he may delay, I will still wait every day for him to come.

...that those who died will be brought to life at whatever time it shall please the Creator, blessed is His Name and exalted is His remembrance forever and for all eternity.

I/5. The Thirteen Middos (character traits) of Rabi Yisrael of Salant

Here are thirteen character traits for a Jew to work on in order to better himself, as suggested by Rabi Yisrael of Salant, the founder of the Mussar movement.

1. **TRUTHFULNESS** [EMES / אֱמֶת]
    Be truthful in all you say.

2. **QUICKNESS** [ZERIZUS / זְרִיזוּת]
    All that you have to do, do without wasting time.

3. **DILIGENCE** [CHARITZUS / חֲרִיצוּת]
    Do all that you are supposed to do conscientiously.

4. **RESPECT** [KAVOD / כָּבוֹד]
    Be extremely careful with the honor and feelings of others.

5. **TRANQUILLITY** [MENUCHA / מְנוּחָה]
    Do everything quietly, without undue confusion or excitement.

6. **GENTLENESS** [NACHAS / נַחַת]
    The words of the wise are spoken softly and peacefully.

7. **CLEANLINESS AND PURITY** [NIKAYON / נִקָּיוֹן]
    Keep your body and your clothing clean and pure.

8. **PATIENCE** [SAVLANUS / סַבְלָנוּת]
    Whatever happens in life, be patient.

9. **ORDER** [SEDER / סֵדֶר]
    Do everything in an orderly and disciplined way.

continued on next page

10. **HUMILITY** [ANAVA / עֲנָוָה]
    Recognize your own faults and weak points,
    but do not dwell on the faults and weak points
    of other people.

11. **RIGHTEOUSNESS** [TZEDEK / צֶדֶק]
    What is hateful to you, do not do unto anyone
    else.

12. **THRIFT** [KIMUTZ / קִמוּץ]
    Do not waste a single penny unnecessarily.

13. **SILENCE** [SH'SIKA / שְׁתִיקָה]
    Judge the value of your words before you
    speak.

I / MISCELLANEA

I/6. Shesh Zechiros — Six Things to Remember

It is a special mitzva to remember and mention the following items. Every morning, after the Shacharis prayers, some people recite the Torah verses in which these items are mentioned.

1. The Exodus from Egypt
   יְצִיאַת מִצְרַיִם

2. The Giving of the Torah at Sinai
   מַעֲמַד הַר סִינַי

3. The evil caused by Amalek and the commandment to destroy him
   מַעֲשֵׂה עֲמָלֵק וּמְחִיָּתוֹ

4. The sins the Jewish people committed in the desert, especially the sin of the Golden Calf
   מַסַּת אֲבוֹתֵינוּ בַּמִּדְבָּר

5. Miriam's deed
   מַעֲשֵׂה מִרְיָם

6. The Sabbath Day
   זְכִירַת שַׁבָּת

I/7. Daily and Holiday Prayers

Shacharis שַׁחֲרִית	The morning prayer
Mincha מִנְחָה	The afternoon prayer
Ma'ariv (Arvis) מַעֲרִיב (עַרְבִית)	The evening prayer
Mussaf מוּסָף	The additional prayer after Shacharis on the Sabbath, Rosh Chodesh, and holidays
Ne'ila נְעִילָה	The closing prayer said at the end of Yom Kippur

I/8. Middos — Measurements

Length
agudal / אֲגוּדָל = approximately the length of a
thumb
tefach / טֶפַח = 4 agudalim (a fist)
ama / אַמָּה = 6 tefachim
mil / מִיל = 2,000 amos
parsa / פַּרְסָה = 4 mil

Volume
beytza / בֵּיצָה = approximately the size of an egg
kezayis / כְּזַיִת = ½ beytza
revi'is / רְבִיעִית = 1½ beytzim
log / לֹג = 6 beytzim
kav / קַב = 4 logim
omer / עֹמֶר = 1.8 kavim
hin / הִין = 1.6 omrim
s'ah / סְאָה = 2 hin
ayfa / אֵיפָה = 3 s'im
kor / כּוֹר = 10 ayfos

Weights
dinar / דִּינָר
sela / סֶלַע = 4 dinar
prass / פְּרָס = 12½ sela
maneh / מָנֶה = 2 prass
kikar / כִּכָּר = 60 maneh

Coins
pruta / פְּרוּטָה
issar / אִסָּר = 8 pruta
pundyon / פּוּנְדְיוֹן = 2 issar
ma'ah / מָעָה = 2 pundyon
dinar (zuz) / דִּינָר (זוּז) = 6 ma'ah
sela (shekel) / סֶלַע (שֶׁקֶל) = 4 dinar
maneh / מָנֶה = 25 sela
(one gold dinar = 25 silver dinar)

I/9. Arba Parshiyos — Four Special Torah Readings

There are four Shabbos mornings in the year when four special, additional sections of the Torah are read. They are...

Parashas Shekalim:
פָּרָשַׁת שְׁקָלִים

To be read on the Shabbos before Rosh Chodesh Adar (or on Rosh Chodesh Adar, if Rosh Chodesh falls on a Shabbos). It tells of the half-shekel each Jew must give to the Beis Hamikdash as his part in the purchase of the year's communal sacrifices.

Parashas Zachor:
פָּרָשַׁת זָכוֹר

To be read on the Shabbos before Purim. Tells of the mitzva to wipe out the memory of the wicked Amalek.

Parashas Parah:
פָּרָשַׁת פָּרָה

To be read on the Shabbos immediately before Parashas Hachodesh. Tells how those who had contact with a dead body must purify themselves before bringing the Pesach sacrifice.

Parashas Hachodesh:
פָּרָשַׁת הַחֹדֶשׁ

To be read the Shabbos before the first of the month of Nissan. Tells us of the importance of the month of Nissan and of its being the first month for counting the months in our year.

I/10. Ten Trials of Avraham Avinu

1. Avraham was commanded to leave the house of his father and go to the Land of Canaan.

2. Avraham was commanded to leave Eretz Yisrael and go to Egypt.

3. Pharaoh, king of Egypt, tried to take Sarah as his wife.

4. Avraham attempted to save his nephew Lot and found himself fighting a savage war against four kings.

5. Sarah brought her servant Hagar to Avraham as a second wife.

6. Avraham was commanded to perform the mitzva of circumcision.

7. Avimelech, the king of the Plishtim, tried to take Sarah as his wife.

8. Sarah told Avraham to send Hagar away.

9. Sarah told Avraham to send his son Yishmael away.

10. Akeydas Yitzchak — Avraham was commanded to bring his son Yitzchak up to the mountain and prepare him as a sacrifice to Hashem.

I/11. Esser Makkos — Ten Plagues

1.	Blood	דָּם
2.	Frogs	צְפַרְדֵּעַ
3.	Vermin	כִּנִּים
4.	Wild Beasts	עָרֹב
5.	Pestilence	דֶּבֶר
6.	Boils	שְׁחִין
7.	Hail	בָּרָד
8.	Locusts	אַרְבֶּה
9.	Darkness	חֹשֶׁךְ
10.	Smiting of the Firstborn	מַכַּת בְּכוֹרוֹת

I/12. Assara Harugey Malchus — the Ten Martyrs

These ten Sages were killed by the Romans during and after the period of the Second Beis Hamikdash.

1. Rabi Yishmael Kohen Gadol
   רַבִּי יִשְׁמָעֵאל כֹּהֵן גָּדוֹל

2. Rabban Shimon ben Gamliel
   רַבִּי שִׁמְעוֹן בֶּן גַּמְלִיאֵל

3. Rabi Akiva ben Yosef
   רַבִּי עֲקִיבָא בֶּן יוֹסֵף

4. Rabi Chananya ben Tradyon
   רַבִּי חֲנַנְיָה בֶּן תְּרַדְיוֹן

5. Rabi Chutzpis Hamesurgeman
   רַבִּי חֲצְפִּית הַמְתַרְגְּמָן

6. Rabi Elazar ben Shamua
   רַבִּי אֶלְעָזָר בֶּן שַׁמּוּעַ

7. Rabi Chanina ben Chachinai
   רַבִּי חֲנִינָא בֶּן חֲכִינַאי

8. Rabi Yeshayvav Hasofer
   רַבִּי יְשֵׁבָב הַסּוֹפֵר

9. Rabi Yehuda ben Dama
   רַבִּי יְהוּדָה בֶּן דָּמָה

10. Rabi Yehuda ben Bava
    רַבִּי יְהוּדָה בֶּן בָּבָא

The End
...but really only the beginning

for the Torah is as deep as the ocean
and as high as the sky —
"longer than the earth
and broader than the sea"* —
and true learning has only a beginning,
but no end.

* Iyov 11:9

Bibliography

Information for parts of this book was taken from the following sources:

Bergman, Meir. *Mevo Shearim.* Israel, 5726.

Bramson, Yosef. *Yemos Olam – Tannaim v'Amoraim.* Jerusalem, 5738.

Carmell, Aryeh. *Aiding Talmud Study.* Jerusalem: Feldheim Publishers, 1986.

The Complete Artscroll Siddur. New York: Mesorah Publications, 1984.

Encyclopedia Judaica. Jerusalem: Keter Publishing, 1972.

Halperin, Yechiel. *Seder Hadoros.* Warsaw, 5637.

Heiman, Aharon. *Toldos Tannaim Va'Amoraim.* Jerusalem: Kirya Neemana, 5724.

Hertz, Joseph H. *Daily Prayerbook.* New York: Bloch Publishing Co., 1955.

Isenberg, Yehuda. *Torah MiSinai.* Jerusalem: Haskel, 1967.

Kol Makom v'Atar. Tel Aviv. Misrad Habitachon and Keter Publishers, 5738.

Midrash Hagadol Bereishis.

MinHahar, Shlomo and Isenberg, Yehuda. *Sheurei Hamitzvos.* Jerusalem: Haskel, 5726.

Rottenberg, Shlomo. *Toldos Am Olam.* Brooklyn: Keren Eliezer, 5727.

Seder Olam Raba.

Siddur Minchas Yerushalayim. "Measurements" by Eliyahu Weissfish. Jerusalem: Hamesorah, 5743.

Siddur Tefillos Yisrael – The Hirsh Siddur. Jerusalem: Feldheim Publishers, 1969.

Sputz, David. *Sefer Shnos Dor Vador.* New York, 5740.

Tal, Shlomo, ed. *Siddur Rinas Yisrael.* Jerusalem: Moreshes Ltd., 1973.

Special thanks ...

First and foremost, to my husband הי״ו . His erudition, optimism, encouragement, and unerring editorial advice leave their mark on everything I write.

To my sons ני״ו — especially Yedidya — who gave so willingly of their time to help compile the information for *The Jewish Factfinder*.

To Rabbi Ben Zion Sobel הי״ו , who used his vast store of Torah knowledge to help verify the myriad details in this book for halachic and factual accuracy. Laborious as this task was, he performed it with his usual good humor and unfailing enthusiasm.

A very special, warm thank you to my good friend Harvey Klineman. Blessed with a wonderful mind and gifted hands, he has graciously and generously applied his rich knowledge and many talents to making this book (and others we have worked on!) better, richer and more beautiful. I am very, very grateful.

ואחרון אחרון חביב ... last, but most certainly not least, my heartfelt thanks to the staff at Feldheim. They are, every one of them, very special.

ויהי נעם ה׳ אלקינו עלינו ומעשה ידינו כוננה עלינו
ומעשה ידינו כוננהו.

תהילים צ